Using Formative Assessment to Support Student Learning Objectives

As student learning objectives become an increasingly prominent approach to setting goals and growth measures in schools, teachers' competence in formative assessment is essential. *Using Formative Assessment to Support Student Learning Objectives* introduces current and future educators to SLOs as tools for shaping career- and college-ready students. Written in concise and straightforward language, and replete with step-by-step exercises, real-life examples, and illustrative charts, this useful guide provides pre- and in-service educators with the theoretical background and practical tools needed to implement the latest SLO research in their classrooms.

M. Christina Schneider is Senior Director of Psychometric Solutions at NWEA and is involved in various federally-funded research projects.

Robert L. Johnson is Professor of Educational Research and Measurement at the University of South Carolina, USA.

Student Assessment for Educators
Edited by James H. McMillan
Virginia Commonwealth University, USA

Using Formative Assessment to Enhance Learning,
Achievement, and Academic Self-regulation
Heidi L. Andrade and Margaret Heritage

Using Students' Assessment Mistakes and Learning
Deficits to Enhance Motivation and Learning
James H. McMillan

Using Feedback to Improve Learning
Maria Araceli Ruiz-Primo and Susan M. Brookhart

Using Self-Assessment to Improve Student Learning
Lois Ruth Harris and Gavin T. L. Brown

Using Peer Assessment to Inspire Reflection and Learning
Keith J. Topping

Using Formative Assessment to Support Student
Learning Objectives
M. Christina Schneider and Robert L. Johnson

For more information about this series, please visit:
https://www.routledge.com/Student-Assessment-for-
Educators/book-series/SAFE

Using Formative Assessment to Support Student Learning Objectives

M. Christina Schneider
and
Robert L. Johnson

Routledge
Taylor & Francis Group

NEW YORK AND LONDON

First published 2019
by Routledge
711 Third Avenue, New York, NY 10017

and by Routledge
2 Park Square, Milton Park, Abingdon, Oxon, OX14 4RN

Routledge is an imprint of the Taylor & Francis Group, an informa business

Library of Congress Cataloging-in-Publication Data
A catalog record for this title has been requested

ISBN: 978-1-138-64950-7 (hbk)
ISBN: 978-1-138-64953-8 (pbk)
ISBN: 978-1-315-62580-5 (ebk)

Typeset in Sabon
by Florence Production Ltd, Stoodleigh, Devon, UK

Contents

Figures

Tables

1

Introduction to Student Learning Objectives

Importance of Formative Assessment for SLOs

Formative assessment practices can guide teachers in making decisions about future instruction. Methods of assessment can include, but are not limited to, anecdotal notes, exit slips, learning logs, think-pair-share activities, and analyzing student work from embedded assessments. When a teacher analyzes evidence of student learning and uses that information to either adjust instruction or provide feedback, he or she is using formative classroom assessment practice (Brookhart, Moss, and Long, 2008). The formative assessment theory of action is based in the idea that a teacher identifies where a child is, determines what the child needs next, and supports the child in closing the gap between where she is and the learning target. The action a teacher takes, however, can increase, decrease, or not influence student learning, depending upon if the action taken was the correct action for that student at that moment in time. This is why researchers have cautioned that formative assessment actions are not accurate and effective unless they result in increases in student learning (Brookhart, 2009; Nichols, Meyers, and Burling, 2009; Shepard, 2009).

Helping teachers learn formative assessment skills is critical to student learning. To understand and monitor student learning over time, however, a teacher cannot focus on the number of correct responses a child is providing. Rather, the teacher must systematically analyze student work to determine if what a child can do represents more sophisticated reasoning and content acquisition than was observed previously. The teacher must recognize that within a single standard is often a range of content- and thinking-skill difficulty that can be measured. This range represents different stages of reasoning. Most important, standards are not objectives that a teacher can check off. Some standards are precursors to other standards, whereas some standards are intended to represent more advanced thinking and summative, year-end expectations. Moreover, grade-level difficulty of some standards is centered in the content of other standards in the same grade. This especially applies in mathematics and science. Therefore, no standard can truly be measured in isolation.

With high quality formative assessment practices, one expects a clear link between the findings of what a child can do currently, what a child needs to be able to do next to meet the learning goal, and what subsequent actions lead to gains in student learning (Nichols, Meyers, and Burling, 2009; Wiliam, 2010). That is, formative assessment practices at their core focus on growth of student knowledge and skills. Teacher actions are intended to be personalized for each student to help the student move his or her own learning forward. Therefore, formative assessment practices are implicitly tied to the goals of the Student Learning Objective (SLO) process that many states now use as the student growth measure.

SLOs, Learning Goals, Growth Targets, Baseline Data, and State Standards

The SLO process is a student-focused goal setting procedure that supports and can improve teacher practice in analyzing student work and using evidence of student learning to take action. The first intended outcome of the SLO process is to measure and support year-long increases in reasoning and content-skill acquisition for all students. To measure these outcomes teachers have to either create or select assessments that measure SLO learning goals. The SLO learning goal is broader and deeper than a learning goal for a single lesson or unit of instruction. It is intended to describe what student proficiency in the content area represents. When the SLO measure is aggregated across students, the second intended outcome for the SLO is commonly a student achievement measure that is used as one indicator in a teacher effectiveness system. SLOs have different components that are typically presented in a state template for teachers to fill out. Table 1.1 defines important terms associated with the SLO process.

Student Learning Objectives Embody Formative Assessment Practices

An SLO is intended to be a student-centered goal setting process. First, the teacher establishes a year-long or course-long learning goal that is essential for students to know and be able to do as they move forward into the next grade or course. The teacher uses this learning goal to collect baseline information about where students are in their learning in the beginning of the year or course, specifies what the outcome of growth looks like for the student, and then monitors student achievement of these growth goals in a formalized, documented process that is specified by the state or district.

SLOs are designed to encourage and support reflective teacher practice. It is the study and reflection about what students can do currently that assists teachers in identifying students who are in different stages of learning. Once the different stages are illuminated, teachers can then determine differentiated instructional actions. When instructional actions are not specifically targeted to a student's needs, student achievement can suffer (Schneider and Meyer, 2012).

States and districts are beginning to require SLOs for all teachers (Hall, Gagnon, Thompson, Schneider, and Marion, 2014;

Table 1.1 Key Components of the SLO Process

Term	Definition	Example
Student Learning Objective Process	The SLO is a student-focused goal setting procedure that is intended to provide a within-year measure of student learning.	Completed templates are available on many state department of education websites, or www.nciea.org/library/recent-publications/slo-toolkit
SLO Learning Goal	The SLO learning goal is an overarching big idea that synthesizes and integrates multiple standards. It requires a year's worth of learning to reach, and it encompasses foundational skills for success in the next grade.	A kindergarten student will use a variety of strategies to add and subtract when presented real-world problems.
Growth Target	The growth target is an individualized student learning goal or "target" that defines the intended growth outcome for students after a year of instruction.	Kindergarten students who began the year in the *Beginning* stage of development will move to *Developing*. They will create a drawing or model to solve addition and subtraction problems presented real-world contexts.
Baseline Data	Baseline data describe where the students are in regard to the SLO Learning Goal prior to instruction. Sometimes, baseline data are collected with a pre-test.	Six kindergarten students are in the *Beginning* stage of the SLO Learning Goal. They can combine and separate sets of manipulatives and then use counting to determine the sum or difference when numbers are within 5.
State Standards	State standards define the grade-level knowledge, content skills, and thinking abilities a state expects students to demonstrate by the end of the year.	www.corestandards.org
Assessment	An assessment is a measurement tool designed, in the SLO context, to measure the SLO Learning Goal.	A series of carefully designed performance tasks that elicit student thinking skills and content knowledge in regard to the SLO Learning Goal.

Lacireno-Paquet, Morgan, and Mello, 2014). South Carolina, for example, has moved from using large-scale assessment data to classroom-based SLOs as a student achievement measure in the teacher effectiveness system because policymakers desire that teachers focus on how to personalize learning for students. When teachers are able to set the learning goals for students and use reflective practices that support formative assessment, they are better able to determine the different learning paths of students in their classroom.

Why Are SLOs Important?

SLOs, when done well, are not additional activities to what an effective teacher does each day. SLOs are tools teachers use to think about what student reasoning looks like along the path of mastering state standards. It is this aspect of SLOs that makes them so valuable. They are essentially classroom-based formative and summative assessment processes that center a teacher's focus on a fundamental theme: What is most important for students to master in a particular grade to be well prepared for the next grade?

Gill, Bruch, and Booker (2013) reported many teachers value SLOs for professional development and planning. High-quality SLOs require a sustained amount of professional development investment in formative assessment techniques and in creating high quality assessments. Given our experience supporting teachers with this process, we find teachers and administrators typically need more than 80 hours of professional development

---

SLO Learning Goal

First grade students will write a short informational paragraph in which they provide facts as elaboration and spell one syllable words correctly with long vowel sounds.

Figure 1.1 Sample Grade 1 SLO Learning Goal

to build the readiness skills that are the foundation for this process.

Just as students need multiple opportunities to learn content before testing, teachers need the opportunity to practice and learn the sophisticated formative assessment skills that underpin the SLO process prior to their official implementation. Many states have not typically required that teachers be formally trained in formative assessment or the creation of high quality assessments (Popham, 2009; Stiggins and Herrick, 2007); yet, this is a skill that is often associated with being a highly-qualified teacher. The SLO process necessitates substantial teacher skill in the collection, interpretation, and triangulation of evidence of student learning. We focus on the development of teacher skills in developing embedded formative assessments that will provide evidence of student learning and methods of analyzing student work for increases in student ability.

SLO Models

No single SLO model has been implemented across the nation. However, it is essential to note that all SLO processes begin with the development of the SLO learning goal. Marion and Buckley (2016) posited that the SLO learning goal should be based upon high leverage knowledge and skills, often referred to as a "big idea" of the discipline. Riccomini, Sanders, Bright, and Witzel (2009) wrote that big ideas should form the conceptual foundation for instruction. Big ideas connect current and future learning with previous learning. Thus, the big idea connects previous, current, and future learning into a learning goal that explicates what cumulative deep, authentic demonstrations of learning look like at the end of the year.

Each SLO model requires that teachers set growth-targets for students based on the SLO learning goal. When setting the growth-target the teacher must consider what the student knows and can do at the beginning of the year, and he or she must make a decision regarding what the expectations for growth will look like for each child. To engage in this process states typically suggest that teachers review baseline data and give pre-tests to students. Baseline data can include previous year large-scale or interim assessment data (if available), classroom grades; Individual Education Plans (IEPs), 504s, English Language learner, gifted and talented status; and possibly even previous year-end samples of work. The idea is that if the teacher has a broad understanding of a student's strengths and weaknesses, the teacher will be better able to pinpoint the student's needs, differentiate instruction, and better determine what the student should be able to do by the end of the current year with good instruction and multiple opportunities to learn.

All SLO models require that teachers interpret historical evidence of student learning and triangulate the historical evidence with the pre-test analysis of student work. While the information gathering process remains similar across SLO models, how growth-targets are defined is the most important difference. In the next section we provide an overview of common SLOs models currently in use and describe challenges of defining and setting growth targets for these models. Finally, we introduce

Table 1.2 Common Elements of SLOs

Guiding Practices
1. SLO processes should begin with the development of an SLO learning goal.
2. The SLO learning goal should be based upon high leverage knowledge and skills, i.e., the "big idea" of the discipline.
3. The big idea should integrate several key content standards.
4. The big idea takes into account previous, current, and future learning to guide the development of a learning goal that explicates what deep demonstrations of learning look like at the end of the year.
5. When setting the growth target the teacher must consider what the student knows and can do at the beginning of the year. The teachers also must make a decision regarding what the expectations for growth will look like for each child.
6. To engage in this process, states typically suggest that teachers review baseline data and give pre-tests to students. Baseline data can include previous year large-scale or interim assessment data (if available), classroom grades, Individual Education Plans (IEPs), and 504s.

the trajectory-based formative assessment SLO process, which supports more personalized learning for students. (Readers who do not desire a review of different SLO models are encouraged to move to the trajectory-based formative assessment SLO section.)

Commercially Available Interim Assessments

In English language arts and mathematics, in particular, there are a variety of commercially available interim assessment products that districts can quickly implement if they want to have standardized achievement measures across a district. These products typically use a vertical scale to support interpreting scale scores over time as a measure of growth. A vertical scale is often created using a common group of items across grade levels. Because scale scores in adjacent grades have relatively similar interpretations, teachers can use the scores to quantify how much a student has learned (i.e., student growth) within or across years. Districts may expect that teachers determine the number of points students should grow on the test scale during the year as the growth-target for one year's worth of learning in the SLO process. That is, the decision-making framework for a growth-target for the teacher may be based on the number of points on the scale a student should increase from the beginning to end of year; however, teachers do not typically have to define the interpretation of what the increase in score points means in terms of a change in reasoning and content skills that are observable in the classroom.

Teacher-Created Multiple Choice Pre-tests and Post-tests

In some districts, teachers (or administrators), either collaboratively or individually, create their own multiple choice pre-test and post-test measures. Using teacher-developed tests helps teachers understand the content that is the target for the assessment. Developed appropriately, these tests are tied to the district curriculum and can provide broad information about instruction and student learning. One of the most important decision points when using this model for SLO purposes is how to construct the pre-test and post-test forms. Considerations in designing these assessments include the following questions:

- Should the pre-test be comprised of items at the grade level of the standards?
- Should the pre-test consist of items that measure precursor skills to determine if students are ready for the demands of the course?
- Should the pre-test be comprised of the same items as the post-test?

The philosophy used to construct the two tests will influence the interpretations regarding what growth means.

Having the same items appear on both tests means student scores might increase because students have already seen the items. That is, the test becomes easier for the students, and the growth teachers observe may be a result of students being familiar with particular items rather than deeper content knowledge. There needs to be a wide range of item difficulties on each form (meaning that you have easy, medium, and difficult items), and the pre- and post-test forms should measure the same content at the same overall difficulty.

Having a wide range of item difficulties on a pre-test is central to understanding *how* students grow and *where* students begin the year in their learning. If some students do well on the pre-test, they have little to no room to show growth. For example, if students respond to 85 percent of the items correctly during the pre-test, the items are too easy for them. Tests that are too easy do not provide enough information about what students need to learn. If the pre-test is too difficult for some students, you do not know where to begin instruction.

Often teachers calculate the percentage of items each student answered correctly on the pre-test and make a prediction regarding the percentage of items students will answer correctly on the post-test. Although this makes intuitive sense, this procedure can only work statistically when items on both pre- and post-test assessments are at the same level of difficulty and measure parallel content. But calculating a percentage correct growth-target does not help the teacher understand *what* change in content knowledge and thinking skills must occur over time. This approach does not describe student growth in terms of observable outcomes that students will develop tied to what is measured on the assessment. Thus, the teacher cannot monitor student progress effectively throughout the year.

Pre-test Post-test Performance Task Model

Teachers who teach writing or the arts commonly use a pre-test post-test performance task model for SLOs. Often the performance task, such as an essay prompt or a piece of music, changes from Time 1 to Time 2. The rubric used to score student work is the same on both occasions in an effort to create the growth interpretation. The first challenge of this approach is that the interpretation of student growth on common rubrics is dependent on the difficulty of the performance task that students receive during the pre-test and post-test. The second challenge is that students in the tails of the distribution of grade-level ability do not have tasks that show what they can do. Task difficulty is central to measuring and interpreting student growth.

To calculate performance task difficulty, find the average rubric score and divide by the number of score points possible on the rubric. For example, if the average score students earned on the rubric is three points and six points are possible, the item difficulty is 0.5. We interpret 0.5 as 50 percent of the students are able to perform the task and 50 percent are not.

In the performance task SLO model, we expect students to improve from Time 1 to Time 2 on the rubric after a year's worth of instruction. However, if the pre-test is at a reduced level of difficulty compared to the second (e.g., 70 percent of the students can perform the pre-test task versus 50 percent of the students can perform the post-test task), it can appear that students did not grow across time. For example, in our experience informational writing is often observed to be easier than argumentative writing on summative assessments because the required writing structure is less complex. If informational writing is used at the pre-test and argumentative writing is used at the post-test, students may have grown in skill beyond the pre-test without reaching the skills needed for the post-test, making it appear that a class did not grow or that they even regressed in skill! In contrast, in the case of the post-test task being easier than the pre-test, it could appear students have made gains when they have not. (Marion, DePascale, Domeleski, Gong, and Diaz-Bilello (2012) write extensively on quality issues in regard to the SLO context for readers interested in this information.)

The pre-test post-test performance task model works best when two tasks of the same difficulty are administered, and the students taking the tasks have skills that are typical of students in the particular grade. However, when a task perfectly targets the center of the student distribution and the class composition has students who are outside of typically developing students, the task will be too hard for low ability students and too easy for high ability students. This conundrum will prevent you from measuring growth.

To measure student ability across *all* students and detect changes in abilities over time, you need multiple interconnected performance tasks that are sequenced by concurrent increases in content difficulty and cognitive demand while simultaneously providing decreases in scaffolding. Easier performance tasks will be just right for low ability students, moderate tasks will be just right for typically developing children, and harder tasks will measure the skills of high ability children at the beginning of the year. The sequence of performance tasks that increase in content and cognitive difficulty during the year allow you to find out what all of your students know in the classroom at the beginning of the year, allow you to progress monitor, and allow you to measure growth across the year because they are designed for this purpose.

Learning Trajectory Formative Assessment Model

Researchers increasingly use learning progressions as the theoretical underpinning for curriculum development, instruction, and assessment. The purpose of using a learning progression in the SLO process is to guide teachers in recognizing and documenting the general developmental pathways of learning. This allows important, rigorous, and content-centered growth targets to be defined. Learning progressions are a tool for teachers. They describe likely learning paths that can guide instruction in a given content area. In this book, we will use the term learning trajectory, consistent with the distinctions in the research literature between learning progressions and learning trajectories (Battista, 2011). Teachers will create the learning trajectories and instructional and assessment tasks based on the curriculum they use in their classroom and district.

Smith, Wiser, Anderson, and Krajcik (2006) defined a learning trajectory as the description of the increasingly more sophisticated ways of reasoning in the content domain that follow one another as a student learns. Clements and Sarama (2014) noted a key characteristic of learning trajectories. They describe students' levels of thinking; not students' abilities to answer a question correctly. Learning trajectories focus on what a child *can* do; that is, learning trajectories describe the ways children's thinking becomes more complex along with the more sophisticated skills and contexts upon which students can demonstrate their understanding.

When children reach the stages representing more sophisticated thinking skills, coupled with more advanced content knowledge, they are reaching the notion of mastery of standards for the grade-level. Being ready for success in the next grade does not mean all items on all assessments must be answered correctly. Rather, it means that particular content, integrated with related standards at higher level thinking skills, must be mastered.

It is the description of the pathway to the specific and integrated content and analyzing student work with respect to that pathway that supports formative assessment practices and clear growth targets. The merger of formative assessment and learning

Table 1.3 Guiding Questions for Developing an SLO

Step	Guiding Question
1	"What do I want my students to know?"
2	"How does student reasoning grow more sophisticated as a child learns?"
3	"What progression of instructional and assessment tasks will support student learning and help me understand my students' thinking?"
4	"What does each student already know?"
5	"What do I need to know about each of my students to support his or her learning?"
6	"How will I know that my students have reached their growth target?"

trajectories is the natural underpinning for the SLO process because SLOs are fundamentally about understanding where individual students are in their learning, providing accurate instructional actions, and supporting students in closing the gap between where they are and the SLO growth target.

Table 1.3 provides questions that will guide you in the SLO process. In the following section, we use Grade 3 Mathematics to provide an overview of the trajectory-based formative assessment SLO model.

Guiding Questions for the Trajectory-based Formative Assessment SLO Model

Step 1: What Do I Want My Students to Know?

In mathematics, multiplication and division concepts are typically introduced in Grade 3 (e.g., for states that use the *Common Core Standards* or adaptations thereof). Multiplication and division are essential building blocks for students' school careers and their own daily lives. There is some debate about whether mathematics curriculums should focus on the rote memorization of "math facts" (e.g., see work by Stanford professor Jo Boaler). However, it is clear from the *Common Core Standards* that students should have a deep conceptual understanding of multiplication, and they need to solve real-world problems that have import to their own lives. Therefore, we might express an SLO learning goal and rationale for Grade 3 mathematics this way:

Learning Goal: Students will conceptualize and justify their responses to multi-step real world and measurement problems that include multiplication and division within 100.

SLO Rationale: Multiplication and division are introduced in Grade 3. These operations are essential building blocks for students' school careers and their own daily lives.

Figure 1.2 Sample Grade 3 SLO Learning Goal

This goal is broad, and it integrates many of the Common Core Grade 3 standards:

- 3.OA.A.1: Interpret products of whole numbers.
- 3.OA.A.2: Interpret whole-number quotients of whole numbers.
- 3.OA.A.3: Use multiplication and division within 100 to solve word problems in situations involving equal groups, arrays, and measurement quantities, e.g., by using drawings and equations with a symbol for the unknown number to represent the problem.
- 3.OA.B.5: Apply properties of operations as strategies to multiply and divide.
- 3.OA.B.6: Understand division as an unknown-factor problem.
- 3.OA.D.8 Solve two-step word problems using the four operations. Represent these problems using equations with a letter standing for the unknown quantity. Assess the reasonableness of answers using mental computation and estimation strategies including rounding.

- 3.MD.C.7.b Multiply side lengths to find areas of rectangles with whole-number side lengths in the context of solving real world and mathematical problems, and represent whole-number products as rectangular areas in mathematical reasoning.
- 3.MD.D.8 Solve real world and mathematical problems involving perimeters of polygons, including finding the perimeter given the side lengths, finding an unknown side length, and exhibiting rectangles with the same perimeter and different areas or with the same area and different perimeters.

Step 2: How Does Student Reasoning Grow More Sophisticated as a Child Learns?

Study this Common Core Standard: 3.OA.A.3 Use multiplication and division within 100 to solve word problems in situations involving equal groups, arrays, and measurement quantities, e.g., by using drawings and equations with a symbol for the unknown number to represent the problem. A teacher may note two things. First, rectangular arrays can be an important center-piece in conceptualizing multiplication and linking multiplication to both repeated addition and area (Confrey, 2010). Second, it is not enough for students to use multiplication and division in isolation in straight computation problems; students must know when to use these operations to solve real-world problems involving equal groups and arrays. If instructional tasks are set up to transition students to move from equal grouping to arrays, teachers can support transitioning student thinking from multiplication as equal shares to generalizing the use of multiplication in other situations such as calculating area. Student modeling is often one of most critical pieces of evidence a teacher can use to determine if the student conceptualizes what the equations represent.

The teacher should note that 3.OA.A.3 does not denote two-step problems. Standard 3.OA.D.8: solve two-step word problems using the four operations, includes two-step problems. The teacher has a decision point. Does 3.OA.A.3 mean that students should solve one-step problems or does it include one-step and two-step problems? Many states restrict this standard to one-step real word problems so it makes sense that 3.OA.A.3 would be a precursor standard to 3.OA.D.8. Thus, students who have mastered 3.OA.A.3 are not yet meeting the overarching SLO learning goal. They are at the learning trajectory stage called *Approaching Target* in Figure 1.3. The *On-Target* stage specifies that students are able to solve two-step real world problems. Between just these two standards we begin to see a concrete example of a pathway to what it means to be proficient in state standards.

The trajectory for the SLO learning goal is called the SLO achievement level descriptor (ALD). The trajectory for the Grade 3 mathematics SLO learning goal is shown in Figure 1.3. All the Grade 3 mathematics standards described in this chapter align to the trajectory.

Step 3: What Progression of Instructional and Assessment Tasks Will Support Student Learning and Help Me Understand Student Thinking?

Performance tasks, sequenced in sophistication based on increases in content difficulty, cognitive demand (critical thinking skills), and conscious contextual choices (e.g., one-step versus two-step problems or with and without visual models), support teachers in understanding where students are in their reasoning skills. SLO ALDs describe the evidence teachers look for to document the child's present level of performance and reasoning in the content area. The trajectory-based performance tasks elicit the evidence regarding what a child can do and his or her thinking.

In the SLO process, trajectory-based performance tasks must be available for instruction and for assessment at each stage of the learning trajectory. That is, the performance tasks representing a stage of the trajectory are created with nuanced differences designed to support and elicit increased reasoning and skill. As the performance tasks grow in difficulty, they

The student	Beginning	Developing	Approaching Target	On Target	Above Target
Conceptualization	Equipartitions manipulatives of odd and even numbers (e.g., 27 divided in 3 groups; 24 divided in 4 groups) and explains equal or fair shares (Confrey et al., 2014)	Places manipulatives within 100 into arrays of more than two to model problems when prompted and explains (verbally or in written form) the relationship between repeated addition and multiplication	Self-creates models within 100 showing arrays to demonstrate the relationship between addition and multiplication	Demonstrates the relationship between multiplication and division within 100	See below
Operations	Adds equal groups of more than two that sum to 100 or less (e.g., 9+9+9)	Solves **single-step** verbal or word problems involving equal groups with factors that are less than or equal to 5. Students in this stage may use repeated addition or recall less difficult facts such as x2 or x3	Uses a variety of strategies to accurately solve **single-step** verbal or word involving equal groups, measurement quantities, area and perimeter when quotients and divisors are less than 100 with factors greater than 5	Solves a variety of **two-step** word problems requiring multiplication within 100 in a variety of contexts including measurement quantities, perimeter and area and factors are greater than 5	Uses relationships between multiplication and division within 144 to solve **multi-step** verbal and word problems involving arrays, and measurement quantities, and the relationship between perimeter and area

Figure 1.3 SLO Achievement Level Descriptor (ALD)

become more complex in terms of the reasoning students must use to solve them. When a teacher believes that the child demonstrates the skills of a particular stage of the trajectory based upon the work observed in the classroom, he or she can administer the SLO performance task to the student to triangulate different pieces of student learning evidence.

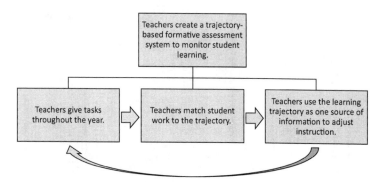

Figure 1.4 Intended Use of Trajectory Based Formative Assessment SLO Model

Let's look at tasks from the conceptualization trajectory.

Stage 1: Beginning. The student equipartitions manipulatives of odd and even numbers (e.g., 27 divided in 3 groups; 24 divided in 4 groups) and explains equal or fair shares (Confrey, Maloney, Nguyen, and Rupp, 2014).

You have 24 chips to fairly share with 4 friends. Use your chips to give each friend a fair share.

Draw what you did.

If one friend leaves, can you share the 24 chips among three friends?

Answer_____

Show how you know.

Draw what you did.

Figure 1.5 Equipartitions Even Number based on Confrey et al., 2014

Stage 2: Developing. The student places manipulatives within
    100 into arrays of more than two to model problems when
    prompted and explains (verbally or in written form) the rela-
    tionship between repeated addition and multiplication.

Put your chips into an array showing 6 groups of 8.

Draw your array.

Write your repeated addition sentence.

Write your multiplication sentence.

How is multiplication connected to addition?

Figure 1.6 Connects Repeated Addition to Multiplication

Stage 3: Approaching. The student self-creates models within 100 showing arrays to demonstrate the relationship between addition and multiplication.

Seven friends have 8 cents each. How much money do they have in all? Show two ways to answer this problem correctly.

Model 1

Model 2

Figure 1.7 Self-Generates Models to Represent Equal Groups and Arrays to Show Relationship Between Repeated Addition and Multiplication

Stage 4: On Target. The student demonstrates the relationship between multiplication and division within 100.

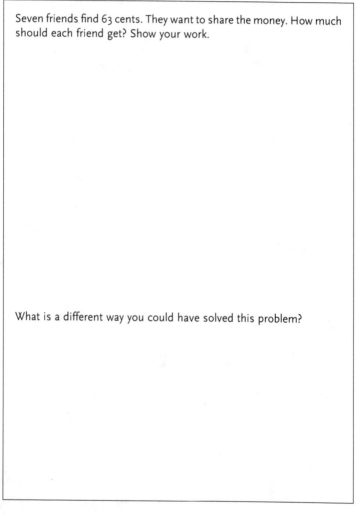

Figure 1.8 Demonstration of the Relationship Between Multiplication and Division

Step 4: What Does Each Child Already Know?

Using teacher judgment, the students are administered different performance tasks that are aligned to their level of development (e.g., Beginning, Developing, Approaching Target, On Target, Above Target). When students do well on a task, they proceed to the next, more difficult task. When students are unable to demonstrate knowledge on a task, they have an easier one. This iterative approach occurs because we are seeking information to locate the child on a learning trajectory that underpins the tasks. It is only when you find what a child can do and cannot do that you know where a child is in their learning and what they need next.

In the trajectory at the Conceptualization – *Beginning Level* the teacher has written that this level is identified by the student equipartitioning "manipulatives of odd and even numbers (e.g., 27 divided in 3 groups; 24 divided in 4 groups) and explains equal or fair shares" (Confrey et al., 2014). Equipartitioning is an action (Wilson, 2014) so in this stage watching what the student is doing is central to understanding the student response.

Figure 1.9 is an example from a Grade 3 student who has already been receiving multiplication and division instruction. The student is responding to a task based on Confrey et al. (2014). We see the student modeled the equipartitioning of an even number of manipulatives for an even number of groups and odd number of groups. The child can be matched to the *Beginning* Stage. Because the match has been made, the child needs the next harder task.

Figure 1.10 is the evidence for the student from the Conceptualize – *Developing Level* descriptor that is designed to show the student "places manipulatives within 100 into arrays of more than two to model problems when prompted and explains (verbally or in written form) the relationship between repeated addition and multiplication." This stage of the trajectory is derived from Grade 2 math standards. The child models an array within each group and shows a repeated addition sentence that matches the model. The child also does not use counting, adding, or build up strategies to solve the repeated addition sentence,

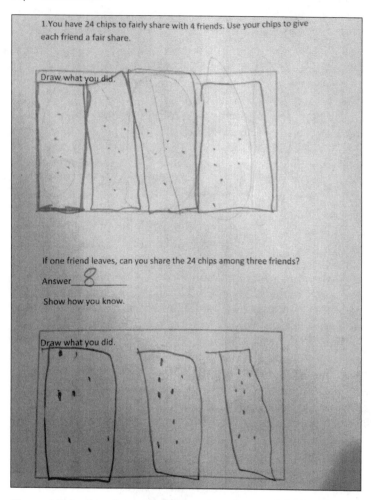

Figure 1.9 Student Response to Conceptualization: Beginning Level Task

and does not show a multiplication sentence connected to the model. The descriptors for the *Developing* level suggest the child should work with arrays and needs to connect repeated addition to multiplication. The student's present level of performance

Figure 1.10 Student Responses to Conceptualization: Developing Level Task

suggests the teacher must start in the related Grade 2 standards that introduce multiplication because the child's thinking cannot yet be matched to the *Developing* level.

Step 5: What Do I Need to Know About Each of My Students to Support His or Her Learning?

As you collect information about student thinking in the content area, it is important to understand other information about the child that influences when and how a student learns, such as his or her family situation, if the student is gifted, or his or her learning style. For example, some students are visual-spatial thinkers (Stretch and Osborne, 2005) who learn best with hands-on projects and highly visual displays of information. Also, some students need highly structured classrooms, whereas others do not.

Teachers should be aware whether students are English language learners, have a 504 plan, or an IEP. What accommodations might a student need to access the curriculum? Students who are behind their peers in reading may need to have texts read aloud in courses outside of reading so that they do not miss having access to the course content. There are many accessibility options using technology, such as iPads that even read Web pages for students simply by invoking the feature!

Step 6: How Will I Know That My Students Have Reached Their Targets?

After creating the learning trajectory, the related performance tasks, collecting pre-test information from students using the performance tasks, and matching student work to the trajectory in the beginning of the year, the teacher has the needed information to identify the child's present level of performance and to set growth targets. The teacher can use the remaining performance tasks to monitor student learning throughout the year.

Briggs et al. (2015), working in Denver Public Schools, used learning trajectories for the SLO process and defined "one year's growth" as movement across two levels of the trajectory. In their work, they defined minimal growth as moving up one level on the trajectory over the course of the year and exceeding growth expectations as moving three or more levels. That is, the child matched to the Beginning Stage (see Figure 1.9) would be expected to move up to the Approaching Target stage by the end of the year if the teacher sets a typical growth target for the student. Briggs et al. noted the advantages of using this approach.

First, the trajectory-based formative assessment SLO process is about understanding where students are at any point in time and thinking about what students need next. This is a process focused on thinking about growth throughout time. It is not a process focused on reaching a certain level of mastery and stopping. Therefore, forward motion is always expected. Because one year's growth is defined as movement across two levels, no matter where you begin the year, the goal for the end of the year is the same for all students: moving across two levels of the trajectory. Briggs et al. noted there is not a penalty for having students who enter a class underprepared because the standardized definition of growth takes into account the student's starting place. Finally, the strongest reason for using a trajectory-based formative assessment approach to SLOs is that teachers have a clear definition regarding the content expectations for each growth target.

Summary

Trajectory-based formative assessment SLOs require teachers to define a big idea (i.e., learning goal) that is central to the discipline. The big idea should be critical for students to learn and fluently use as they move forward in their education in subsequent grades. Teachers then define how student knowledge and skills grow more sophisticated during the year as they reach, and also exceed, the learning goal. Once the trajectory is established, rich performance tasks are developed to elicit the evidence that students have reached a stage of the trajectory and also to help facilitate learning opportunities for them to learn those skills. These tasks supplement, rather than supplant, what the teacher is doing during instruction and with the curriculum.

The trajectory-based performance tasks teachers use in the classroom also allow them to check that tasks embedded into the curriculum rise to high enough levels to capture students who are working slightly above grade level. The use of these tasks, along with matching student work to the SLO ALD (the trajectory) allows teachers to see the range of student needs in their classroom. It also supports teachers in ensuring that they are not consistently bombarding a student with work that is much too advanced or too easy.

By collecting multiple pieces of evidence of student work representative of a stage on the trajectory, the student's present level of performance in relation to the SLO ALD can be triangulated, which supports more reliable teacher inferences about student reasoning, and this information can be used to personalize instruction to address the student's need and to progress monitor. This process works when teachers have support and training in analyzing student work, but this support must not be overlooked because researchers have found many teachers need support with this skill (Heritage, Kim, Vendlinski, and Herman, 2009; Schneider and Gowan, 2013). When analyzing authentic samples of student work based on what students can do becomes the focus of the SLO process, teachers begin to transition to a formative assessment lens.

As Heritage (2008) described, teachers may find they need to go further back in a progression to clear up misconceptions or to fill gaps in students' knowledge that are preventing them from meeting the year-long learning goal. Additionally, teachers of students whose content and reasoning are more advanced than that of their peers have information to support this conclusion and can focus instruction on developing the students' thinking to higher levels of cognitive and content demand, which may mean going beyond the student's current grade-level curriculum. In using this approach, growth is not a number. The growth-target decision-making framework is a description of the thinking skills and content that students need to master. In the next chapter the process for determining the SLO learning goal will be described.

References

Battista, M. (2011). Conceptualizations and issues related to learning progressions, learning trajectories, and levels of sophistication. *The*

Mathematics Enthusiast, 8(3), 507–570. Retrieved May 7, 2018, from http://scholarworks.umt.edu/tme/vol8/iss3/5

Briggs, D.C., Diaz-Bilello, E., Peck, F., Alzen, J., Chattergoon, R., and Johnson, R. (2015). *Using a learning progression framework to assess and evaluate student growth.* Center for Assessment, Design, Research and Evaluation (CADRE) and National Center for the Improvement of Educational Assessment. Retrieved May 7, 2018, from www.colorado.edu/education/sites/default/files/attached-files/CADRE.CFA-StudentGrowthReport-ExecSumm-Final.pdf

Brookhart, S., Moss, C., and Long, B. (2008). Formative assessment. *Educational Leadership, 66*(3), 52–57.

Brookhart, S.M. (2009). Editorial. *Educational Measurement: Issues and Practice, 28*(3), 1–3.

Clements, D.H., and Sarama, J. (2014). Learning trajectories: Foundations for effective, research-based education. In A.P. Maloney, J. Confrey, and K.H. Neuyen (Eds.) *Learning over time: Learning trajectories in mathematics education.* Pp. 1–30. Charlotte, NC: Information Age Publishing.

Confrey, J. (2010). Response commentary. *Journal of Urban Mathematics Education, 3*(2), 25–33.

Confrey, J., Maloney, A.P., Nguyen, K.H., and Rupp, A. (2014). Equipartitioning, a foundation for rational number reasoning: Elucidation of a Learning Trajectory. In A.P. Maloney, J. Confrey, and K.H. Neuyen (Eds.) *Learning over time: Learning trajectories in mathematics education.* Pp. 61–96. Charlotte, NC: Information Age Publishing.

Gill, B., Bruch, J., and Booker, K. (2013). *Using Alternative Student Growth Measures for Evaluating Teacher Performance: What the Literature Says.* REL 2013-002. Regional Educational Laboratory Mid-Atlantic.

Hall, E., Gagnon, D., Thompson, J., Schneider, M.C., and Marion, S. (2014). State practices related to the use of student achievement measures in the evaluation of teachers in non-tested subjects and grades. NCIEA. Retrieved May 7, 2018, from www.nciea.org/library/state-practices-related-use-student-achievement-measures-evaluation-teachers-non-tested

Heritage, M. (2008). *Learning progressions: Supporting instruction and formative assessment.* CCSSO. Washington, DC.

Heritage, M., Kim, J., Vendlinski, T., and Herman, J. (2009). From evidence to action: A seamless process in formative assessment? *Educational Measurement: Issues and Practice 28*(3), 24–31.

Lacireno-Paquet, N., Morgan, C., and Mello, D. (2014). *How states use student learning objectives in teacher evaluation systems: A review of state websites*. Washington, DC: US Department of Education.

Marion, S.F. and Buckley, K. (2016). Design and implementation considerations of performance-based and authentic assessments for use in accountability systems. In H. Braun (Ed.) *Meeting the challenges to measurement in an era of accountability*. Pp. 49–76. Washington, DC: NCME.

Marion, S., DePascale, C., Domaleski, C., Gong, B., and Diaz-Bilello, E. (2012). Considerations for analyzing educators' contributions to student learning in non-tested subjects and grades with a focus on student learning objectives. *Center for Assessment*. Retrieved May 7, 2018, from www.nciea.org/library/considerations-analyzing-educators-contributions-student-learning-non-tested-subjects-and

Nichols, P.D., Meyers, J.L., and Burling, K.S. (2009). A framework for evaluating and planning assessments intended to improve student achievement. *Educational Measurement: Issues and Practice, 28*(3), 14–23.

Popham, J. (2009). Assessment literacy for teachers: Faddish or fundamental? *Theory Into Practice, 48*(1), 4–11.

Riccomini, P., Sanders, S., Bright, K., Witzel, B.S. (2009). 20 ways to facilitate learning experiences through differentiated instructional strategies. *Journal on School Educational Technology, 4*(4), 7–14.

Schneider, M.C., and Gowan, P. (2013). Investigating teachers' skills in interpreting evidence of student learning. *Applied Measurement in Education, 26*(3), 191–204.

Schneider, M.C., and Meyer, J.P. (2012). Investigating the efficacy of a professional development program in formative classroom assessment in middle school English language arts and mathematics. *Journal of Multi-disciplinary Evaluation, 8*(17), 1–24.

Shepard, L.A. (2009). Commentary: Evaluating the validity of formative and interim assessment. *Educational Measurement: Issues and Practice (28)*3, 32–37.

Smith, C.L., Wiser, M., Anderson, C.W., and Krajcik, J. (2006). FOCUS ARTICLE: Implications of research on children's learning for standards and assessment: A proposed learning progression for matter and the atomic-molecular theory. *Measurement: Interdisciplinary Research & Perspective, 4*(1–2), 1–98.

Stiggins, R.J. and Herrick M. (2007). A status report on teacher preparation in classroom assessment. Unpublished research report. Portland, OR: Classroom Assessment Foundation.

Stretch, L.S., and Osborne, J.W. (2005). Extended time test accommodation: Directions for future research and practice. *Practical Assessment, Research & Evaluation, 10*(8), 1–8.

Wiliam, D. (2010). Standardized testing and school accountability. *Educational Psychologist, 45*(2), 107–122.

Wilson, P.H. (2014). Learning trajectories and professional development. In A.P. Maloney, J. Confrey, and K.H. Neuyen (Eds.) *Learning over time: Learning trajectories in mathematics education*. Pp. 227–242. Charlotte, NC: Information Age Publishing.

2

Developing the SLO Learning Goal

The SLO learning goal is the enduring understanding that students should possess by the end of the course or the school year to be successful in the next grade. Marion and Buckley (2016) recommended that the learning goal for an SLO be based upon high leverage knowledge and skills, often referred to as a "big idea" of the discipline, and embody several key content standards. When developing the SLO learning goal, the teacher must investigate how separate but related standards and skills converge over time and the best methods for obtaining proof that a student's content skills and thinking are increasing in complexity. In this chapter, we focus on the first salient question a teacher must ask while creating the SLO framework for the year.

1. "What do I want my students to know?"
2. "How does student reasoning grow more sophisticated as a child learns?"

3. "What progression of instructional and assessment tasks will support student learning and help me understand student thinking?"
4. "What does each child already know?"
5. "What do I need to know about each of my students to support his or her learning?"
6. "How will I know that my students have reached their target?"

What Do I Want My Students to Know? — The SLO Learning Goal

Defining the appropriate grain size, or level of detail, that is appropriate for the SLO learning goal is central to the SLO process. The National Center for the Improvement of Educational Assessment (2013) wrote that creating a high-quality SLO learning goal requires the development of a description of the "big idea" that grows from the beginning to end of year by synthesizing

- the most critical content and skills from the state's standards and district's curriculum,
- appropriate instructional strategies,
- necessary time span to teach the SLO learning goal, and
- how the learning goal will be measured.

Table 2.1 provides examples of SLO learning goals that provide descriptions of student understandings that are too large to provide a focused goal, too small to encompass a year's worth of expected learning, and appropriately integrated goals that build upon multiple standards. The exemplars are intended to synthesize multiple standards, are measurable, require a year's worth of learning to reach, and encompass foundational skills for success in the next grade.

The SLO learning goal is intended to help the teacher focus on the most critical content and skills from the state's standards and district's curriculum that are essential for student success in the next grade. That is, with many standards to teach, what is the year-long theme (big idea) that is introduced in the beginning of the year, develops and grows during a year, and by the end of the year is observed as underlying more sophisticated skills in the discipline? This theme is an enduring understanding upon which multiple standards contribute and to which they connect.

The big idea is often found connected to penultimate standards (e.g., "3.MD.D.8 Solve real world and mathematical problems involving perimeters of polygons, including finding the perimeter given the side lengths, finding an unknown side length, and exhibiting rectangles with the same perimeter and different areas or with the same area and different perimeters," which was part of our example in Chapter 1). Exhibiting rectangles with the same perimeter and different areas requires understanding the connection of multiplication to the use of arrays in area models, and students need to be fluent in multiplication strategies to efficiently exhibit rectangles in the manner that the standard specifies.

The SLO big idea as an enduring understanding can be seen in the SLO learning goal examples in Table 2.1. Teachers observe kindergarten students for the practical application of key phonics skills as the students read grade-appropriate texts and write to communicate. These phonics rules of the English language need to be automated and in place by the end of kindergarten, so in first grade students are ready to learn more complex strategies to support their independent reading and writing. Grade 8 mathematics students are demonstrating skills in real-world problem contexts and are solving and graphing two linear equations with two variables. The use of real world contexts is important because this requires students to analyze how to solve a problem rather than implement a procedure without context. Linear equations are precursor knowledge to nonlinear equations in upper level math courses. Thus, these SLO learning goal choices are purposeful.

The SLO learning goal must be measurable, and it should necessitate that students engage in authentic *demonstrations* (i.e., performance tasks) of their thinking and learning in real-world contexts. These demonstrations provide *visible* or aural evidence of the students' current level of performance, provide opportunities to integrate skills from multiple standards, and allow teachers to witness student thinking in action. Because we want more complex demonstrations of student learning, several standards underpin the SLO learning goal. Therefore, in the examples we provide, we typically include multiple actions we expect students to demonstrate.

Table 2.1 Example SLO Learning Goals

Too Large	Too Small	Appropriately Integrated Goals
Kindergarten students will read grade appropriate texts.	Kindergarten students will pronounce the initial, medial, and final sounds in a three-phoneme word.	Kindergarten students will apply phonics rules for one-syllable words with a short vowel sounds to decode unfamiliar words as they read grade-appropriate texts and encode words as they write.
Grade 8 Mathematics students will solve functions.	Grade 8 Mathematics students will graph linear functions of real-world and mathematical situations.	Grade 8 Mathematics students will solve and graph systems of two linear equations in two variables in real-world problems.
Grade 8 Social Studies students will synthesize social studies information to make inferences and draw conclusions.	Grade 8 Social Studies students will explain the primary motivations for English colonization of the New World.	Grade 8 Social Studies students will infer causes of points of view regarding minority's rights over time in the United States based upon evidence from primary source documents and historical context.
Grade 8 band students will compose music.	Grade 8 band students will perform seven major scales.	Grade 8 band students will notate and perform short compositions in major tonality and triple meter.

The phrasing of the SLO learning goal should include explicit, action verbs that a teacher elicits from students. How we elicit student thinking is covered in our chapter on performance tasks. What is important for the creation of the SLO learning goal is the choice of explicit action verbs such as critique, write, solve, perform, draw, and show. For example, in Table 2.1, for the "Appropriate" section for Grade 8 band, the explicit verbs are "notate and perform." Teachers should avoid generic implicit and internal action verbs such as know, understand, or recognize. Interested readers can see Mehrens and Lehmann (1991) for other examples of clarifying language that support measuring student knowledge, skills, and reasoning. In addition to action verbs, SLO learning goals should contain the key content competencies a student should demonstrate by the end of the year. Thus, in the kindergarten example the key content competency relates to one syllable words with the short vowel sounds, or in the Grade 8 Mathematics example we see two linear equations. Let's take a more in-depth look at how we synthesize multiple standards into an SLO learning goal.

Synthesizing Multiple Standards into an SLO Learning Goal

In this example, the SLO learning goal is intended to connect and integrate multiple English language arts standards. The explicit action verbs in the SLO learning goal are *use* and *write*. The content competencies involve digital sources and informational texts.

SLO Learning Goal

Grade 3 students will use information from digital sources and multiple texts to write their own informational texts on a topic that they choose.

Figure 2.1 Example Grade 3 SLO Learning Goal

The following standards connect to the SLO learning goal and are sequenced to support the development of skills over time. Students will use the first cluster of listening and reading skills specified in the standards to support informative writing as a component of the SLO learning goal. The use of listening and reading standards is purposeful. Listening to content related to an informational topic assists students in reading more advanced vocabulary. It also allows students who are in earlier stages of reading development to acquire sufficient content to engage in the writing task that is the central focus of the SLO learning goal. It is the information a student uses when writing and how that writing is organized that the teacher will use as evidence to draw a conclusion that the student is able to meet the SLO learning goal. We sequenced the Common Core standards as follows:

- "Determine the main ideas and supporting details of a text read aloud or information presented in diverse media and formats, including visually, quantitatively, and orally."
- "Determine the main idea of a text; recount the key details and explain how they support the main idea."
- "Use information gained from illustrations (e.g., maps, photographs) and the words in a text to demonstrate understanding of the text (e.g., where, when, why, and how key events occur)."
- "Compare and contrast the most important points and key details presented in two texts on the same topic."
- "Describe the relationship between a series of historical events, scientific ideas or concepts, or steps in technical procedures in a text, using language that pertains to time, sequence, and cause/effect."
- "Write informative/explanatory texts to examine a topic and convey ideas and information clearly."
  - Introduce a topic and group related information together; include illustrations when useful to aiding comprehension.
  - Develop the topic with facts, definitions, and details.

- – Use linking words and phrases (e.g., also, another, and, more, but) to connect ideas within categories of information.
- – Provide a concluding statement or section.
- – Write informative/explanatory texts to examine a topic and convey ideas and information clearly.

Notice that when we sequence and connect the standards we also are illuminating key differences in expectations of student thinking. The first three standards become precursor skills to comparing and contrasting, and these comparison skills are central to understanding and analyzing sequence and cause/effect in texts or about topics that influence the child's ability to describe (and more importantly infer) relationships in a series of historical events, scientific ideas, or concepts. Finally, students need to be able to engage in these skills as they conduct research to support drafting and organizing their own informational texts.

As you consider creating your own SLO learning goals, think about how standards can be organized so that one standard is a precursor to another. Copy or print your state standards. Cut them out, and place them in a sequence. Organizing and documenting this sequence can help you think about how skills develop and accumulate across a year and which standards (or parts of standards) may represent more advanced stages of reasoning than others. It is the more advanced stages of reasoning and more complex content that often bridge the current year to the next subsequent year. This exercise can be useful in refining what you really intend with your SLO learning goal. You might also be thinking that doing this work with a team of teachers would be useful, and we agree.

Nuances of SLO Goals Across Content Areas

A guiding recommendation for creating an SLO learning goal is that it should comprise the most critical content and skills from the state's standards and district's curriculum that are essential to master for the next grade. However, this recommendation can be more challenging in some content areas than others. This requirement is most easily met in English language arts and mathematics because the standards are generally created by states to build upon each other over time. However, some content areas such as social studies, for example, may not have standards that are structured in a way to easily see paths of growth.

Standards that structure student learning outcomes as specific to particular pieces or units of information (e.g., a time period in history or specific content pieces in science) rather than recursive themes across time become more difficult to consolidate into the SLO process unless literacy standards or scientific inquiry skills are considered. For example, the South Carolina Social Studies Academic Standards (2011) define content understandings within periods of time such as this Grade 8 example, "The student will demonstrate an understanding of the causes of the American Revolution and the beginnings of the new nation, with an emphasis on South Carolina's role in the development of that nation" (p. 63). This standard and its corresponding sub-standards are too specific to a unit of instruction to serve the purpose of the SLO. However, South Carolina also has a literacy standard, "Evaluate multiple points of view or biases and attribute the perspectives to the influences of individual experiences, societal values, and cultural traditions" (p. 63). It is the literacy standard that history teachers can and should cultivate over the course of the year because evaluating bias is necessary when analyzing primary source documents, no matter the time period of their origin.

The analysis of primary source documents for an author's perspective is an enduring understanding of the discipline from middle school to the university level. An SLO learning goal such as "Grade 8 Social Studies students will infer causes of points of view regarding a minority's rights over time in the United States based upon evidence from primary source documents and historical context," allows a teacher to connect historical themes such as repression and civil and political rights across time periods in terms of experiences of Native Americans,

African-Americans, women, immigrant populations, and the lesbian, gay, transgender, and bisexual community. Such an SLO learning goal also allows students to draw their own conclusions about causes and effect relationships and make their own connections.

In most content areas it makes sense for the SLO learning goal to focus on explicit action verbs such as critique, write, solve, perform, and apply, such as those in Webb's Depth of Knowledge framework (Webb, 2005). Webb's framework is designed to help educators understand the reasoning skills students must use when engaging in content area tasks. The framework can also be used to understand the reasoning expectations of standards, and this framework is often used by states when they align items on the state assessment to standards. Because most states use an alignment policy model that 50 percent of a test's items have to be aligned at or above the cognitive level of the state standard (Webb, Herman, and Webb, 2007), it makes sense that teachers ensure SLO learning goals meet or exceed the cognitive expectation that appear in the state standards. However, for some courses such expectations may not be appropriate.

Nuances of SLO Goals in Arts-Related Courses

For disciplines such as dance and physical education, particularly in the early stages of development, it may not be appropriate to focus on the cognitive verbs in the SLO learning goal. Because the big idea of the discipline in dance introductory courses or in early elementary school targets learning spatial and temporal movements, one would expect to see the learning goals centered in learning to automate foundational movements in the discipline. Similarly, for the teachers who see their students a relatively few times a year, such as the arts teachers in elementary school, the grain size of their SLO learning goals will understandably be smaller than those from teachers who see students each day.

One of the core tenets of SLO learning goal construction from the National Center of Improvement of Educational Assessment (2013) is that the learning goal must be feasible and in the teachers' power to effect change. We would not expect a first-grade teacher to successfully teach reading to students based upon 40 minutes of reading instruction each week. Similarly, it is not feasible to expect an elementary music teacher who teaches first-grade students to teach reading music under this same scenario. Thus, the grain size of the first-grade music SLO learning goal, by necessity, must be small and should be the most important learning goal for the year. Optimally, teachers should meet and discuss grain sizes of SLO learning goals and compare SLO learning goals *across grades and teachers*. This evaluation and collaboration is a powerful method of finding out what teachers feel is important for students to learn and to develop consistent expectations about the grain size of SLOs within a school or district. This is part of a robust SLO learning goal development process.

The SLO Learning Goal Planning Sheet

To help guide you in the process of creating your SLO learning goal, complete the SLO learning goal planning sheet. This planning sheet is intended to be a precursor task to completing the SLO template your state and/or district requires as part of their documentation of the SLO. While this chapter demonstrates this process with Grade 3 English language Arts, Chapter 1 demonstrates the process with Grade 3 mathematics.

Summary

The SLO learning goal establishes the foundation within a classroom about the key content and skills that students must synthesize over the course of instruction to be successful in the next grade. That is, the SLO learning goal should take students roughly a year to master. Therefore, it is optimal that the SLO learning goal be based upon high leverage knowledge and skills that are most important for the students to learn, and it should integrate several key content standards. As you develop SLO learning goals, it may be helpful to use the *SLO Learning Goal*

Student Learning Objective (SLO) Learning Goal Planning Sheet

Grade Level	SLO Content Area
SLO Interval of Instruction *Choose One* ☐ Year ☐ Semester	**SLO Frequency of Instruction** *Choose One* ☐ Each day ☐ Two or Three times a week ☐ One time a week or less

I. **SLO Learning Goal Draft:** Review your standards and think about how your curriculum is structured. What are the most important skills that students need to demonstrate to be successful in the next grade? What is your evidence to support your conclusion that this is the right SLO Learning Goal?

II. **Standards:** Write the standards that connect to your draft SLO Learning Goal.

III. **Sequence Standards:** Organize and sequence these related standards to work together, to support the growth of the "big" idea" skill over time. Highlight the key standards that represent the most sophisticated levels of thinking. Cutting out the standards to sequence them may be helpful as you engage in this process.

IV. **Deep Demonstration:** Describe what deep demonstrations of student thinking in relation to the SLO learning goal look like. Consider especially how the standards highlighted above intersect with those demonstrations. What do you need to see students do to draw the conclusion they have met the SLO learning goal?

V. **SLO Learning Goal Almost Final:** Draft a revision of your SLO learning goal after considering deep demonstrations of student thinking and sequencing the standards. Remember this goal is the enduring understanding that students should possess at the end of the course or the year to be successful in the next grade.

Figure 2.2 SLO Learning Goal Planning Sheet

VI. **Gather Peer Feedback:** Ask colleagues to review your almost final SLO learning goal for feedback against the SLO Learning Goal Criteria. Include teachers who teach the same content at the next higher grade. You may need to reach out to other teachers in your district if you are the only person in your school who teaches the content (e.g., visual arts teacher) at your school.

VII. **SLO Learning Goal Criteria:** Compare your learning goal to the following criteria.

- ✓ Your SLO learning goal is measurable; it includes explicit, action verbs.
- ✓ Your SLO learning goal requires that students engage in deep demonstrations of their thinking in the content area.
- ✓ Your SLO learning goal contains the key content competencies a student should demonstrate by the end of the year.
- ✓ Your SLO learning goal connects and integrates multiple critical standards that are central to the discipline. You have documented evidence to support this claim.
- ✓ Your SLO learning goal will elicit student reasoning at or above the cognitive demand levels denoted by single state standards in isolation.
- ✓ Your SLO learning goal grain size is appropriate to the amount of instructional time you have with the students.

VIII. **SLO Learning Goal Final:** Draft your final version of your SLO Learning Goal in your District/State SLO template. Transfer your sequenced standards to the SLO template. Once these two things have been done, you are ready to draft your SLO learning goal rationale in your District/State template, and you are ready to create your SLO trajectory.

Figure 2.2 continued

Planning Sheet as you go through the following thought processes and actions:

1. Analyze the standards. Which subset of standards work together to build student understandings that are most central to the discipline and form a "big idea"?
   a. Can you find research evidence, citations in the literature, or evidence from your school's data to support your conclusions? These pieces of evidence are useful to support your thinking, and they form the foundation for your rationale when you complete an SLO template that your state or district specifies as documentation of the SLO.
2. Draft the SLO learning goal. Next, document the standards that connect to it. Organize and sequence these related standards to work together, to support the growth of the "big idea" over time.
   a. Do you find critical skills that should be learned by the end of the year that integrate and subsume earlier standards, and thus are standards of greater import in terms of defining what year-end success looks like? Should you edit the SLO learning goal based upon what you have found?
3. Visualize what deep demonstrations of student thinking and work look like for the SLO learning goal. What do you need to see students do to draw the conclusion they have met the SLO learning goal? Is what you visualize represented by the explicit measurable verbs in your SLO learning goal, and represented by higher DOK levels based upon Webb's methodology? We will discuss Webb's reasoning levels more in Chapter 3.
4. Share your learning goal with teachers who teach your content area in the next higher grade and in the grade that you teach. Do these teachers agree that these skills are central to students being successful in their class?
5. Finally, check one last time that your SLO learning goal meets these criteria.
   ✓ Your SLO learning goal is measurable; it includes explicit, action verbs.

✓ Your SLO learning goal requires that students engage in deep demonstrations of their thinking in the content area.

✓ Your SLO learning goal contains the key content competencies a student should demonstrate by the end of the year.

✓ Your SLO learning goal connects and integrates multiple critical standards that are central to the discipline. You have evidence to support this claim documented.

✓ Your SLO learning goal will elicit student reasoning at or above the cognitive demand levels denoted by single state standards in isolation.

✓ Your SLO learning goal grain size is appropriate to the amount of instructional time you have with the students.

Once you have completed the process described in this chapter you are ready to create your SLO trajectory as described in the next chapter.

References

Marion, S.F. and Buckley, K. (2016). Design and implementation considerations of performance-based and authentic assessments for use in accountability systems. In H. Braun (Ed.) *Meeting the challenges to measurement in an era of accountability.* Pp. 49–76. Washington, DC: NCME.

Mehrens, W.A. and Lehmann, I.J. (1991). *Measurement and evaluation in education and psychology.* Fort Worth, TX: Harcourt Brace College Publisher.

National Center for the Improvement of Educational Assessment. (2013). *Instructional guide for developing SLOs.* Dover, NH: Author. Retrieved from www.nciea.org/wp-content/uploads/3_Instructional-Guide-for-Developing-Student-Learning-Objectives.pdf

South Carolina Department of Education (2011). *South Carolina social studies academic standards.* Columbia, SC: Author.

Webb, N.L. (2005). *Web alignment tool (WAT): Training manual. Draft Version 1.1.*

Webb, N.M., Herman, J.L., and Webb, N.L. (2007). Alignment of mathematics' state-level standards and assessments: The role of

reviewer agreement. *Educational Measurement: Issues and Practice,*
26, 17–29.

Wisconsin Center for Education Research, Council of Chief State School
Officers. Retrieved September 15, 2005, from www.wcer.wisc.edu/
wat/index.aspx.

3

Creating the SLO Learning Trajectory

Once the SLO learning goal has been developed and refined, the next step is for a teacher to make explicit his or her interpretation regarding what growth means for the SLO learning goal over time. That is, the teacher should describe the evidence he or she needs to see to draw a conclusion that a child is in a particular stage of development. Learning trajectories describe the ways children's thinking becomes more complex with more difficult content along with contexts in which students can demonstrate their understanding. Because descriptions of children's thinking and learning along a related, often hypothesized, route of instructional and assessment tasks are depicted (Clements and Sarama, 2004) in the SLO *achievement level descriptor* (ALD), teachers should determine how some standards can be precursors for others. This notion of sequencing standards as precursors to other standards was introduced in Chapter 2. In this chapter, we extend this notion to thinking about how within-grade sequencing of standards intersects with standards from adjacent grades and how the tasks we give students can be reflective of easier or more sophisticated stages of thinking. The focus of this chapter is the second salient question a teacher should ask while creating the SLO framework for the year.

1. "What do I want my students to know?"
2. **"How does student reasoning grow more sophisticated as a child learns?"**
3. "What progression of instructional and assessment tasks will support student learning and help me understand student thinking?"
4. "What does each child already know?"
5. "What do I need to know about each of my students to support his or her learning?"
6. "How will I know that my students have reached their target?"

Content Difficulty, Context, and Cognitive Demand: Key Ingredients for SLO ALDs

Content Difficulty

On a large-scale assessment, how do students in one level of achievement differ in knowledge, skills, and abilities than students in the next higher level? To answer this question, Schneider, Huff, Egan, Gains, and Ferrara (2013) investigated items on a large-scale mathematics assessment to determine what made items easier or more difficult for students than others. They compared content across the achievement levels, which are the categories that provide the interpretation of each scale score, such as Level 2, Level 3, and Level 4. Grade 4 students scoring in Level 1 were typically able to add one-digit numbers, whereas students scoring in Level 2 were typically able to add three-digit numbers. Students scoring in Level 3 were typically able to add decimals, and students scoring in Achievement Level 4 were typically able to add whole numbers with fractions.

There are two important findings from this study that apply to SLOs. First, the mathematical content was becoming increasingly more difficult and conceptually complex as achievement levels increased. Second, while the Common Core Standards have "Fluently add and subtract multi-digit whole numbers using the standard algorithm" as an expectation, this skill was not sufficiently difficult enough to be considered a "Level 3 skill" on the assessment.

On a large-scale assessment, proficiency is often predicated on students' mastering and synthesizing multiple skills by the end of the year. Students would be expected to have mastered adding and subtracting multidigit whole numbers early in the Grade 4 year. This is likely because students begin adding and subtracting two-digit numbers in Grade 2 and continue to expand to multi-digit numbers in Grade 3. From a curriculum perspective, adding multi-digit numbers may be a precursor skill necessary for students to learn prior to adding decimals. For Grade 4 students, however, this skill may not be a sufficiently difficult task for the state to consider that a student is synthesizing the most important skills in Grade 4. That is, adding multi-digit numbers in Grade 4 is expected to be easier for students because they have had more practice across years. To be considered Level 3 (or Proficient) requires more difficult content (adding decimals and adding fractions) that are important for students to learn to be successful in Grade 5, and Grade 4 teachers have to build student knowledge of decimals and their relationships to fractions conceptually over a period of time. Therefore, just as you did when thinking about SLO learning goals, creating trajectories requires that you think about the sequence of content and the difficulty of that content.

Another consideration when creating trajectories is that tasks targeting one standard can be easier or more difficult based on the content embedded in the task from another standard. For example, Schneider et al. (2013) found Grade 8 students who could calculate unit rate based on a word problem with a two-digit and one-digit number scored in the Level 3 category; whereas Grade 8 students who could calculate unit rate based on a word problem with two, two-digit numbers scored in the Level 4 category. Another way to think about this is that unit rate problems can be easier if using one-digit numbers with no real-world problem context and more difficult if the task comprises two-digit and one-digit numbers situated in a real-world context. If this idea is extended, it can be inferred that solving for a unit rate presented in a real-world problem context with three-digit and two-digit numbers is the task with the highest difficulty for these students. Thus, thinking about these nuances is important when considering what it is we want students to know by the end of the year, what mastery means, and how skills grow based on more difficult content.

Context

Egan, Schneider, and Ferrara (2012) posited that to create high quality trajectories teachers have to consider the context in which a skill is being measured. Context is the condition under which a child can demonstrate a particular skill. A child may be able to calculate unit rate; however, this skill demonstration is dependent on whether the child is asked to perform the skill in isolation or as a part of a word problem with two or three steps. Subtle nuances in content difficulty influence when a child is successful in showing what he or she can do along with the scaffolding that may or may not be embedded into tasks. This occurs because scaffolding that may provide additional support in understanding the task or content difficulty nuances (mathematical problem versus word problem) can reduce or elevate the cognitive demand of the task. Asking a child to calculate the area of a shown figure given a particular content difficulty (e.g., the width and length are both two-digit numbers) is likely to be less difficult than asking the same type of question with no figure shown. This is because without the model, the student must be able to visualize the figure. This applies to both mathematics and science. The number of concepts and processes that students must integrate to respond to the task must be monitored and made explicit because this affects the difficulty of the task as do tasks that elicit higher levels of the Webb Depth of Knowledge (DOK; Webb, 2005) framework (Ferrara and Steedle, 2015).

Cognitive Demand

Webb's (2005) DOK framework is designed to help educators understand the reasoning skills students must use when engaging in content area tasks. These reasoning skill levels also are a focus of attention when creating learning trajectories as the higher the DOK level of the task, the more complex thought processes we expect to occur. The stages are summarized as follows for mathematics and science. Interested readers should review the chapter on performance tasks to see examples for English language arts or reference Webb's freely available training manual.

Teachers transforming SLO learning goals into SLO learning trajectories (often called SLO ALDs) have to investigate the expected demonstrations of mastery from the previous grade. The sequence of grade-level content (how the SLO learning goal can be measured based on easier and more difficult content), the context in which tasks are situated, and cognitive demand of tasks all serve as supports as you articulate how student thinking becomes more sophisticated as students increase in ability along an SLO trajectory.

Sequence of Grade Level Content

Turning back to English language arts, consider this standard and what it does and does not tell you, as shown in Table 3.2.

- "Write informative/explanatory texts to examine a topic and convey ideas and information clearly.
    - Introduce a topic and group related information together; include illustrations when useful to aiding comprehension.
    - Develop the topic with facts, definitions, and details.
    - Use linking words and phrases (e.g., also, another, and, more, but) to connect ideas within categories of information.
    - Provide a concluding statement or section."

Table 3.1 DOK Definitions

Level 1: Recall and Retrieval Knowledge	Level 2: Conceptual Understanding	Level 3: Strategic Thinking	Level 4: Extended Thinking
Level 1 tasks elicit recall of information stored in one's long-term memory such as facts, definitions, and procedures or retrieval of explicit information from a graph or a text. Straight computation or a one-step, straight-forward mathematics problem are also examples of a Level 1 task, even when presented as a word problem.	Level 2 tasks elicit some decision making, inference, or application when solving a problem, and include the use of number skills, visualization skills, and probability skills. Level 2 tasks include observing, inferring, and explaining patterns; collecting; classifying, organizing, comparing, and plotting data in tables, graphs, and charts; and comparing ideas and concepts and making connections in texts.	Level 3 tasks elicit some strategic planning, reasoning, inference, and often require using evidence to support and explain justifications. Level 3 tasks include drawing conclusions from observations, developing propositions for concepts using evidence, deciding which concepts to apply, and showing multiple pathways to a solution with problems that typically have more than one step.	Level 4 tasks elicit complex reasoning, planning, processes, and thinking over a period of time such as multiple classes or weeks. Level 4 tasks require integrating conceptual understanding, higher-order thinking, and solutioning such as designing, conducting, writing, and critiquing experiments, oral histories, and short stories.

Note. For more information see the "Web Alignment Tool (WAT): Training Manual" and Powerpoint by N. Webb (2005), from http://wat.wceruw.org/index.aspx

Table 3.2 What the Standard Does and Does Not Suggest

Does Suggest	Does Not Suggest
Student writes to convey information	Whether the topic is based on personal expertise, historical events, scientific ideas or concepts, or steps of a technical procedure
Students should group related information together and categories (subtopics) of information should be present	If understanding of content grouping is from information learned from doing, information learned from listening, information learned through reading
Students should write more than one paragraph	How many paragraphs are expected

Donovan and Smolkin (2011) depicted multiple development paths after researching student writing skills for informational writing that likely applies to student writing in the elementary grades. Their ideas applied to a grade-level SLO ALD format is shown in Table 3.3. Across the elementary grades these same stages and strategies for writing (for example a fact list) can generally be observed; however, the length of the student response tends to grow as grade increases. That is, a Grade 2 student and Grade 4 student can be in the same "Fact List" stage; as shown in Figure 3.1 and Figure 3.2. Generally, Grade 4 students will write a fact list using simple sentences with compound verbs or nouns, whereas Grade 2 students will write a fact list using simple sentences.

The SLO ALD based on the work of Donovan and Smolkin (2011) articulates the output (the student writing). It does not describe the input: the source material for the informational text. Across content areas, the input (what specifically a child is asked to do), however, can influence the difficulty of a task based upon the content difficulty, the number of concepts or processes required for students to integrate, and the DOK level. For

Table 3.3 Informational SLO ALD Based on Donovan and Smolkin (2011)

Fact List	Fact List Collection	Couplet Collection	Single and Unordered Paragraphs	Ordered Paragraphs
Students write two or more simple sentences on a topic for which order of presentation is not important.	Students write fact lists for two or more subtopics connected by a larger topic for which order of the presentation is not important.	Students write two or more related sentences on a subtopic connected by a larger topic for which subtopic order is important. The relationships often include statement reason, statement/example.	Students introduce topic and subtopics that contain three or more sentences. The subtopics presentation order is not important.	Students write implied paragraphs that introduce topic and subtopics. The implied paragraphs cannot be rearranged without altering meaning unless through connecting words and transition sentences.

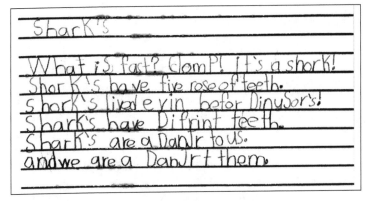

Figure 3.1 Fact List Informational Text by a Grade 2 Student

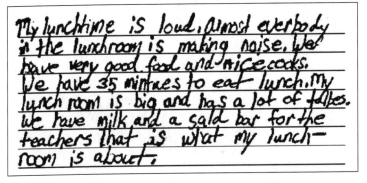

Figure 3.2 Fact List Informational Text by a Grade 4 Student

Source: U.S. Department of Education, Institute of Education Sciences, National Center for Education Statistics, National Assessment of Educational Progress (NAEP), 2002 Writing Assessment

example, the Grade 4 student is writing an informational text on a familiar experience, i.e., a lunchroom experience, whereas the Grade 2 student is writing an informational paragraph, not from personal experience, but rather based upon a topic the child chose and for which the child has read multiple books with support.

Task Difficulty

The Grade 3 Writing standard "Write informative/explanatory texts to examine a topic and convey ideas and information clearly" does not elaborate on the scenarios upon which students compose their text; however, Donovan and Smolkin (2002) noted that children can write more organizationally cohesive informational texts for some tasks than others. How the student gains access to the content about which they are writing influences the difficulty of the task. For example, if a student is learning about new information from reading, there is a need to engage in reading comprehension processes prior to developing their own informational text. Broadly speaking, students have to engage in both the reading process and the writing process. Students who have difficulty with the first process, comprehending the text, acquire less content knowledge on a topic making it more difficult to write a more organizationally developed text.

Below are examples of informational writing tasks that range from easy to more difficult.

Easy: Tasks that ask students to write an informational text on a topic of interest. To frame the task, the teacher might ask students to write an informational text on something about which they know a great deal. Such a task is easier for students because they are able to focus on the writing process based upon information they already know. They are retrieving and organizing information from memory. The task input is at a DOK 1, students are retrieving or recalling information from memory. The task output, the writing sample, is a DOK 3 because students are synthesizing and organizing the information in writing.

Moderately easy: Tasks that ask students to summarize an informational text on a topic from a book a teacher has read aloud several times. Cummins and Stallmeyer-Gerard (2011) described that students need explicit instruction on how to move forward from recalling facts (i.e., Donovan and Smolkin's fact list stage) to how facts work together to convey a big idea. Cummins and Stallmeyer-Gerard's work can help teachers support students as they summarize main ideas, and they provide nice examples of student work that generally align with the trajectory developed by Donovan and Smolkin (2011). Summarizing an informational text a student has heard several times is more complex than the previous task. Before writing students have to determine the main ideas and supporting details of the text they listened to and then organize the information to share it in writing. Here, students engage in listening and writing. The task input is at a DOK 2, students determine the main idea and likely retrieve explicit details to support the main idea. It could be possible that this is a DOK 3 listening task, depending upon if students are retrieving implicit details or making connections across details to support an implied main idea. The task output, the writing sample, is at a DOK 3 because students are synthesizing and organizing the information in writing and hopefully making generalizations when they do so.

Moderately Difficult: Tasks that ask students to summarize key points of a topic based on informational text from a book and from either a read-aloud or a video clip on a topic a teacher assigns a child to do independently. Here the child needs to transfer the synthesis skills learned from the read-aloud stage to using those same skills when reading a book independently coupled with a video clip on the same topic. This task is more complex than the previous task because students have to first decode the text prior to determining the main idea and supporting details of the text. The task input is at a DOK 2, students determine the main idea and likely retrieve explicit details to support the main idea. The task output, the writing sample, is a DOK 3 task because students are synthesizing and organizing the information in writing, and hopefully again making generalizations when they do so. For students who have trouble with this task, the teacher cannot be sure which process is breaking down; the reading process or the writing process. When the read aloud task is the precursor task with a successful response, and a child is unsuccessful when asked to read independently, the teacher is able to determine the reading process is where the breakdown occurred for the child.

Difficult: Tasks that ask students to create an informational book on a topic of teacher choice after reading multiple books independently and listening to a video clip on the topic. With this task the child needs to transfer the synthesis skills from reading a book to determine the main idea to using those same skills when reading multiple books to gain information on the larger topics and subtopics. Once again there is an increase in the information students must process (i.e., focusing on a larger topic with connected subtopics; comparing important points and key details in different texts on the same topic) and students are engaging in work at a DOK level of 4 for both the input and output because the work must occur over an extended period of time for each component.

Highly Difficult: Tasks that ask students to create an informational book on a topic of student choice after reading multiple books independently and listening to a video clip on the topic. Here the child needs to transfer the synthesis skills from researching and creating a book on a topic and subtopics to gain information on a larger topic and subtopics that a student is interested in learning about. There is less structure provided to the student so the child is moving to independently researching a topic. Once again students are engaging in work at a DOK level of 4 for both the input and output because the work must occur over an extended period of time for each component.

Of key importance for this SLO framework is that standards do not express the nuances that move students from novice to more advanced stages of development as shown in Table 3.2. To create the SLO ALDs means you need to sequence standards and then consider what makes tasks easier and more difficult for students within a single set of related standards. These nuances need to be built into the trajectory. Because a student's attitude toward writing affects his or her writing achievement (e.g., Graham, Berninger, and Fan, 2007), it makes sense that helping a child be successful on easier tasks prior to moving her to more difficult tasks is a key ingredient for supporting positive attitudes toward writing and growth in writing skills. Trajectory-based performance tasks support positive attitudes and growth in writing, and they are addressed in more detail in Chapter 4.

Students need instructional supports based upon where they are in their own development. For this reason, the SLO ALD can include expectations about what the teacher will do to move the student forward that is individualized to the student's level of development. You are establishing descriptors of what a student can do as well as what the teacher should do to support the student's growth.

SLO Trajectory Development Guidelines

Table 3.4 summarizes the steps in developing an SLO trajectory. In the following section, we use kindergarten content standards related to phonics to provide an overview of the development process.

Table 3.4 Steps for Developing an SLO Learning Trajectory

Steps
1. Define the SLO learning goal.
2. Study the grade level standards that support the SLO learning goal.
3. Study the off-grade level standards that relate to the SLO learning goal.
4. Review the curriculum materials, both on and off grade.
5. Sequence the standards and content in terms of difficulty for students considering when the content is taught and the cognitive processes students use to complete the tasks.
6. Merge standards into the SLO ALD considering differences in content, cognitive demand, and context across stages.

Step 1: Define the SLO Learning Goal

The first step in creating the SLO ALD is to define the SLO learning goal. Let's use this example.

> Kindergarten students will apply phonics rules for one syllable words with a short vowel sound to decode words when reading highly decodable texts and to encode words when writing.

This SLO learning goal integrates reading and writing standards, and it implies that the teacher will focus on the systematic explicit phonics instruction found to be critical (Ehri, Nunes, Stahl, and Willows, 2001) in teaching a majority of children to read and in preventing reading deficits. The SLO learning goal also implies that the teacher will use texts that provide abundant decoding practice opportunities such as those found online at www. textproject.org/beginningreads. Decodable texts are texts that have a high percentage of words that are phonetically regular and comprise letter sound relationships that have been previously taught (Cheatham and Allor, 2012). Cheatham and Allor concluded in their review of research that students need adequate time to learn decoding skills in order to apply them as a reading strategy; therefore, the purpose of the SLO learning goal is to ensure students have a firm foundation in applying the letter sound relationships when reading and writing.

We recognize some reading teachers in kindergarten will be concerned the SLO learning goal focuses on explicit phonetics based instructional outcomes, rather than learning other standards related to reading (e.g., recognizing high frequency words). It is important to share our rationale. In our experience, first grade teachers prefer that children enter first grade being able to decode CVC (consonant-vowel-consonant) words, and they are less focused on sight words than many kindergarten teachers might suspect. Second, Ehri (2002) noted that teaching sight words to students who do not yet understand the alphabetic principle (i.e., all the letters and sounds in words are connected) can interfere with a child's reading development. That is, if children are taught sight words too soon, they do not learn to attend to all letter-sound relationships in a word, and they are more likely to remain inaccurate, disfluent readers and spellers. Finally, while early reader texts often encourage students to determine the word from the illustration, this is a strategy that struggling readers continue to use in higher grades. Therefore, based on research evidence we suggest decodable texts are essential to use first so students have sufficient practice in decoding. When students show evidence that decoding is becoming automated, they are demonstrating the alphabetic principle. Students then have the readiness to acquire sight words rapidly into their reading vocabulary. They are also ready to use illustrations to support decoding as an early stage entry into using context clues when reading connected text.

Step 2: Review the Grade Level Standards That Support the SLO Learning Goal

Standards typically define the minimum a student should know at the end of the year. However, standards do not present clear descriptions of how students' learning progresses in a domain over the course of the year (Heritage, 2008), and they do not describe how standards must be synthesized in order for students to be ready to succeed at the next grade. Teachers should determine which grade level standards best support the SLO learning goal. On-grade standards for supporting the phonics skills in the SLO learning goal are shown in Table 3.5.

Table 3.5 On-Grade Common Core Standards to Support the SLO Learning Goal

Kindergarten
Recognize and name all upper- and lowercase letters of the alphabet.
Blend and segment onsets and rimes of single-syllable spoken words.
Isolate and pronounce the initial, medial vowel, and final sounds (phonemes) in three-phoneme (consonant-vowel-consonant, or CVC) words. (This does not include CVCs ending with /l/, /r/, or /x/.)
Add or substitute individual sounds (phonemes) in simple, one-syllable words to make new words.
Demonstrate basic knowledge of one-to-one letter-sound correspondences by producing the primary sound or many of the most frequent sounds for each consonant.
Associate the long and short sounds with the common spellings (graphemes) for the five major vowels.
Distinguish between similarly spelled words by identifying the sounds of the letters that differ.
Use a combination of drawing, dictating, and writing to compose informative/explanatory texts in which they name what they are writing about and supply some information about the topic.

Step 3: Study the Above- and Below-grade Level Standards That Relate to the SLO Learning Goal

In kindergarten, the Common Core standards can be merged into a trajectory; however, it takes analyzing both the kindergarten and first grade standards to define the expectations for kindergarten students. Notice that students in kindergarten should associate long and short sounds of vowels with their common spellings, but, the common spellings that drive the long vowel sound are more specifically articulated in Grade 1. Students who are advanced in a grade can generally do most of, but not all of, the things at the current grade. In addition, advanced students are already accessing much of the content in the next grade. So, the student who can demonstrate 1 to 1 letter sound correspondence for consonant letters, short sounds for vowels, decode and encode CVC words, and decode words with a final -e while reading is likely an advanced kindergarten child. Therefore, the kindergarten trajectory must integrate not only standards from the current grade but also the grade above and below as relevant to describing what the student can do.

Step 4: Review On and Off Grade Curriculum Materials

It is important to review the sequence of instructional materials and the exit outcomes for the grade to determine the degree of alignment between the bridging points of the learning trajectory across grades. How the materials connect with previous grade and subsequent grade expectations are called bridging points. Bridging points are important for differentiating among children who, for example, are functioning at the expectations for the grade and those children who are exceeding expectations.

By the end of kindergarten—and throughout the year—students will be in different stages of phonemic awareness and reading development that need to be measured. SLO ALDs need to follow both the students' learning development and the skills and strategies expressed in the standards. In a typical year-end

Table 3.6 On-Grade and Off-Grade Standards to Support the SLO Learning Goal

Kindergarten	*First Grade*
Recognize and name all upper- and lowercase letters of the alphabet.	
Blend and segment onsets and rimes of single-syllable spoken words.	Orally produce single-syllable words by blending sounds (phonemes), including consonant blends.
Isolate and pronounce the initial, medial vowel, and final sounds (phonemes) in three-phoneme (consonant-vowel-consonant, or CVC) words. (This does not include CVCs ending with /l/, /r/, or /x/.)	Isolate and pronounce initial, medial vowel, and final sounds (phonemes) in spoken single-syllable words.
Add or substitute individual sounds (phonemes) in simple, one-syllable words to make new words.	Segment spoken single-syllable words into their complete sequence of individual sounds (phonemes).
Demonstrate basic knowledge of one-to-one letter-sound correspondences by producing the primary sound or many of the most frequent sounds for each consonant.	Know the spelling-sound correspondences for common consonant digraphs.
Associate the long and short sounds with the common spellings (graphemes) for the five major vowels.	Know final -e and common vowel team conventions for representing long vowel sounds.
Distinguish between similarly spelled words by identifying the sounds of the letters that differ.	
Use a combination of drawing, dictating, and writing to compose informative/explanatory texts in which they name what they are writing about and supply some information about the topic.	Write informative/explanatory texts in which they name a topic, supply some facts about the topic, and provide some sense of closure.

early reader connected text often associated with Fountas and Pinnell (2010) Level C or D or Beaver and Carter's (2017) *Development Reading Assessment* level 4 or 5, the student must apply phonics-based rules with final -e and early consonant blends, particularly the "st" and "th" sounds. These two skills are explicitly found in the Grade 1 standards. If the teacher only focuses on the standards and does not look at the phonics-based expectations from the reading system a district or school uses to determine if a child's reading is "on track" for first grade, important skills a child needs to be taught could be omitted unintentionally from instruction. For this reason, teachers must look at standards, curriculum, and expected student outcomes to create the SLO ALD.

Step 5: Sequence the Standards and Content in Terms of Difficulty

The trajectory is the hypothesized route of instructional and assessment tasks that increase in difficulty and sophistication (Clements and Sarama, 2004). At this stage teachers should re-sequence the standards into an order that shows how some standards are precursors for others within the target grade that is being taught and the adjacent grades. The teacher should also begin to look at the verbs in the standards. Verbs that are implicit should be made explicit to begin defining how the teacher knows that the child is demonstrating the skill. That is the SLO ALD should describe the type of evidence he or she will see in authentic responses of student work in order to draw the conclusion the student is able to demonstrate the skills. The teacher should also begin thinking about adding more specificity about the contexts in which the student is demonstrating the tasks. For example, if a child is pronouncing individual sounds (phonemes) in short vowel, one-syllable words, it is time to determine if these are CVC words (e.g., hat, mat, sat) or CV-ck words (duck, luck, muck) and how these content differences affect the difficulty of the tasks for students in terms of the progression.

Table 3.7 On-Grade and Off-Grade Standards Resequenced and Edited to Support the Kindergarten SLO Trajectory

Kindergarten	First Grade
Name and write all upper- and lowercase letters of the alphabet.	
Identify onsets and rimes of single-syllable spoken words.	Encode single-syllable words by blending sounds (phonemes), including consonant blends.
Say the primary sound or the most frequent sounds for each consonant.	
Pronounce the initial, medial vowel, and final sounds (phonemes)in three-phoneme (consonant-vowel-consonant, or CVC) words.[1] (This does not include CVCsending with /l/, /r/, or /x/.)	Pronounce initial, medial vowel, and final sounds (phonemes) in spoken single-syllable words.
Pronounce individual sounds (phonemes) in simple, one-syllable words that differ in similarly spelled words.	Produce 1 to 1 spelling-sound correspondences for common consonant digraphs (st, sh, ch, th and wh).
Encode similarly spelled CVC, CVCC (e.g. duck, spell) words by identifying the sounds of the letters that differ.	Decode final -e and common vowel team conventions for representing long vowel sounds.
Associate the long (final -e) and short sounds with the common spellings (graphemes) for the five major vowels.	Encode single-syllable final -e and common vowel team words into their complete sequence of individual sounds (phonemes).
Use a combination of drawing, dictating, and writing to compose informative/explanatory texts inwhich they name what they arewriting about and supply someinformation about the topic.	Write informative/explanatory texts in which they name a topic, supply some facts about the topic, and provide some sense of closure.

Step 6: Merge Standards into the Trajectory Considering Differences in Content, Cognitive Demand, and Context Across Stages

The last step is moving the skills into a trajectory that describes the content students are able to demonstrate while carefully considering what makes content easier or more difficult for students as they grow in their skills. Content difficulty can be based upon the complexity of the tasks as described earlier in this chapter, the genre of texts students must read or produce, the relative number of steps a student must reason through to solve a problem, the use of familiar versus unfamiliar scenarios, and the vicinity of supporting details for tasks (i.e., are they clustered together or sparsely spread in the text).

Of key import when developing trajectories is to refrain from use of terms such as partially demonstrates, adequately demonstrates, and consistently demonstrates or any method of counting as defining phrases to separate stages of development. Trajectories are not centered in counting how often or defining a percentage of responses a child answers correctly. Rather, they are describing what the child is demonstrating when given content for high leverage standards. Creating trajectories is about looking at what a child is actually doing and considering the sophistication of the task. Consider the following example from a Grade 2 math class that illustrates this point.

> A teacher gives a pre-test on adding and subtracting two-digit numbers and comparing number sentences that use two-digit and three-digit numbers. A student answers the sections on adding and subtracting two-digit numbers correctly. On the last section, however, rather than place greater than or less than symbols in the answer boxes for comparing number sentences, the student has placed an equal sign for each number pair. The teacher marks all of the student's responses in this last section incorrect. She writes a score of 85 percent at the top of the paper, and she concludes the student needs to be placed into this unit of instruction.
>
> However, a second teacher on closer inspection investigates *why* the child missed the section on the comparing number sentences, and she discovers the student has marked the two sides as equivalent

Table 3.8 Final Version of Kindergarten SLO Trajectory

First Stage	Second Stage	Third Stage	Fourth Stage	Fifth Stage	Sixth Stage
Name all upper- and lowercase letters of the alphabet	Pronounce 1 to 1 letter-sound correspondence for each consonant; write upper- and lowercase consonants when teacher provides the sound	Produce 1 to 1 letter-sound correspondence for each short vowel sound; write upper- and lowercase vowels when teacher provides the sound	Produce sounds that differ between similarly spelled CVC words; encode similarly spelled CVC words during dictation; decode CVC words independently when reading early decodable readers	Produce 1 to 1 sound correspondence for st, sh, ch, th and wh; encode cvc words accurately when expressing thoughts in informative texts	Decode consonant digraphs st, sh, ch, th, wh independently when reading; encode one-syllable words that have consonant digraphs with short vowel sounds; decode and encode one-syllable words with short vowel sound followed by –ck or with a double f,l,s,z in authentic reading and writing scenarios; decode one-syllable words with a finale -e

for each question because the student has balanced the two sides, either adding to or subtracting from one of the sides to make it equivalent to the other. The child is not only demonstrating understanding of greater than or less than, the child is showing a beginning awareness of algebraic concepts! The child is demonstrating more advanced reasoning and needs more difficult tasks to grow her thinking skills in the content area. Remaining in the unit for instruction will not grow the child's skills!

This example illustrates when we count correct responses (or incorrect responses) without looking at the content and actual contexts of tasks we miss student thinking. We have to analyze what a child is doing on what type of content in the classroom, and we have to describe increases of student thinking on more difficult content in the trajectory. This is why, when developing the final version of the trajectory, you must also attend to the DOK level that is embedded into the SLO ALD stages and how these relate to the implied DOK levels of the standards. SLO ALDs have to describe the evidence of the cognitive demand with which students are engaging in the content. If a state defines its standards as the cumulative expectation for students cognitively, then this expectation should be depicted in the trajectory by holding the cognitive level constant across stages while the rigor of the content increases. Most states expect tasks to be created above the cognitive demand of the standards (this is what is done on many statewide large scale assessments) in the higher stages of the SLO ALD. In this case, you will likely need to increase the cognitive level across stages while also increasing the difficulty of the content. This idea is shown earlier in this chapter when describing the inputs of easier and harder writing tasks.

Finally, when developing the final version of the trajectory you need to attend to contextual or scaffolding characteristics that need to be present in order for the student to demonstrate the skill. For example, students may be able to access informational texts when that text has organizational structures or graphics that help the student locate and interpret the information. Without such scaffolds, the student may not be able to independently re-read and locate the necessary details to fully comprehend the information that in turn will influence the ability to write coherently on the topic.

If you review the SLO ALD in Chapter 1, there are contextual descriptions in the *Developing* level of the mathematics trajectory, "Solves *single-step* verbal or *word* problems involving equal groups with factors that are less than or equal to 5. Students in this stage may use *repeated addition or recall less difficult facts* such as x2 or x3." The SLO ALD describes the context of the task (single-step word problems) and the predominate strategies students use to solve the problems. Also note the SLO ALD stipulates the word problems may be given either verbally or in print.

Stipulating that word problems may be given either verbally or in print promotes many positive outcomes. First, you are giving access to the curriculum and assessments to students who have not yet developed their reading skills to the degree necessary to access real-world problems in print. Second, this allows the descriptors from your SLO ALD to also be used on a student's IEP as an appropriate measurable goal. This encourages collaboration with resource teachers to support the child's learning.

Reading is a threshold skill to access the content beginning in approximately Grade 3. Students with lower levels of reading achievement or print-based learning differences can often not learn what they need to or demonstrate what they know as they get older because of reading deficits. Thus, denoting problems given in print or verbally in the SLO ALD ensures students are getting the accommodations they need to engage meaningfully in the mathematics work. Also, the teacher is ensuring that he can document what his students have learned. If the teacher holds students with reading deficits entirely to representations of mathematics solely based in print, we can expect that the teacher will see little growth over the year in terms of what students can do. In turn, this will also lower the effectiveness measure of the teacher. Finally, verbal presentations of mathematics also allow the teacher to capture authentic moments in time in which any student might ask and answer his or her own real-world mathematics problems in side bar conversations that the teacher later documents. These examples of students thinking mathematically with problems that are meaningful to their own lives represents the most compelling evidence that students are retaining and transferring the content from the class.

The SLO ALD Planning Sheet

To assist you in the process of creating your SLO ALD, complete the SLO ALD planning sheet to guide your thinking. This planning sheet is intended to be a precursor task to completing the SLO template your state and/or district requires as part of their documentation of the SLO. While this chapter demonstrates this process with English Language Arts, Chapter 1 shows an SLO Trajectory for Grade 3 mathematics.

Summary

The SLO process is designed to support teachers in conceptualizing what it means for students to grow by focusing teachers on the enduring understandings that students should possess at the end of the course or the year of instruction to be successful in the next grade. After defining the "big idea" that multiple standards imply, the teacher (or optimally teams of teachers) develops a trajectory that describes the content, context, and cognitive demand of the evidence they will collect, and what teachers should look for in student work to determine where a child is in their content skill acquisition process.

The SLO ALD provides a framework for teacher decision-making regarding how to best support student learning. In the beginning of the year it is not unusual to discover some students are in early stages of reasoning in the content while others are highly advanced. For students in the middle, they are served by a teacher's typical instructional pace. However, for students in earlier stages of content reasoning, the typical instructional pace will be too difficult because it moves too quickly for them. For students who are more advanced, the typical instructional pace will move too slowly. Neither of these groups will have their needs met unless we can personalize what we do to support them. Using the trajectory-based formative assessment SLO

SLO ALD Planning Sheet

Grade Level	SLO Content Area	
I. **SLO Learning Goal Final:** Write the SLO Learning Goal here.		
II. **Standards:** Document across-year standards that to work together, to support the growth of the "big idea" skill over time.		
Previous Year Standards that are precursor skills to Current Grade Standards for the "Big Idea."	Current Grade Standards sequenced to support the "Big Idea."	Subsequent Year Standards that are next steps to Current Grade Standards for the "Big Idea."

III. **Review Below Grade, On Grade, and Above Grade Curriculum Materials:** Review the sequence of instructional materials and aspired exit outcomes for the previous grade and entry points of the next higher grade to determine the degree of alignment between the bridging points of the learning trajectory across grades. Bridging points are how the materials connect with previous grade and subsequent grade expectations. Write down important findings that help you clarify what should happen in the grade you teach.

Figure 3.3 SLO ALD Planning Sheet.

IV. **Sequence and Edit Standards:** a) Sequence standards and content in terms of difficulty for students considering when the content is taught and the cognitive processes students use to complete the tasks, b) change verbs that are implicit to explicit action verbs, and c) add specificity about the contexts in which the student is demonstrating the tasks (what are the tasks' inputs).

V. **Merge Standards into the SLO ALD:** Merge standards into the trajectory considering differences in content, cognitive demand, and context across stages.

Stage 1	Stage 2	Stage 3	Stage 4	Stage 5

VI. **SLO ALD Criteria:** Compare your SLO ALD to the following criteria.

✓ Your SLO ALD connects and integrates multiple critical standards that are central to the discipline within grade and intersects with standards in the previous and next subsequent grade in the beginning and advanced stages.

✓ Your ALD focuses on what students can do at each stage.

✓ Your ALD articulates evidence that students are increasing in content skill and critical thinking from one stage to another.

✓ Your ALD defines differences in content across stages rather than the frequency (e.g., no use of often, sometimes, or counting) with which students respond to content.

✓ Your ALD describes the contextual or scaffolding characteristics needed so a student can demonstrate the skill.

✓ Your ALD increases in cognitive processing complexity across levels in a cogent way.

✓ Your ALD provides a mental picture of increases in skill across levels.

Figure 3.3 continued

approach, the teacher-developed growth target for each of these students will be dependent upon where the child is currently and where along the trajectory the teacher sets as the year-end learning goal. With the related set of instructional tasks and assessments that serve as multiple opportunities to learn discussed in the next chapter this process encourages and supports teachers as they learn to identify when students are in different stages of learning and to take differentiated instructional actions based on student needs.

References

Beaver, J., and Carter, M. (2017). *Developmental reading assessment* (2nd ed. Plus). London: Pearson.

Cheatham, J., and Allor, J. (2012). The influence of decodability in early reading text on reading achievement: A review of the evidence. *Reading and Writing, 25*(9), 2223–2246.

Clements, D.H., and Sarama, J. (2004). Learning trajectories in mathematics education. *Mathematical Thinking and Learning, 6*(2), 81–89.

Cummins, S., and Stallmeyer-Gerard, C. (2011). Teaching for synthesis of informational texts with read-alouds. *The Reading Teacher, 64*(6).

Donovan, C., and Smolkin, L. (2002). Children's genre knowledge: An examination of K-5 students' performance on multiple tasks providing differing levels of scaffolding. *Reading Research Quarterly, 37*(4), 428–465.

Donovan, C., and Smolkin, L. (2011). Supporting informational writing in the elementary grades. *The Reading Teacher, 64*(6), 406–416.

Egan, K.L., Schneider, M.C., and Ferrara, S. (2012). Performance level descriptors: History, practice and a proposed framework. In G. Cizek (Ed.) *Setting performance standards: Foundations, methods, and innovations* (2nd ed.). Pp. 79–106. New York: Routledge.

Ehri, L. (2002). Phases of acquisition in learning to read words and implications for teaching. In R. Stainthorp and P. Tomlinson (Eds.) *Learning and teaching reading.* London: British Journal of Educational Psychology Monograph Series II.

Ehri, L.C., Nunes, S., Stahl, S.A., and Willows, D.M. (2001). Systematic phonics instruction helps students learn to read: Evidence from the National Reading Panel's meta-analysis. *Review of Educational Research, 71*(3), 393–447.

Ferrara, S., and Steedle, J. (2015). Predicting item parameters using regression trees: Analyzing existing item data to understand and improve item writing. *Paper presented at the annual meeting of the National Council of Measurement in Education*, Chicago, IL.

Fountas, I.C., and Pinnell, G.S. (2010). *Fountas and Pinnell benchmark assessment system 1. Grades K–2, levels A-N*. Portsmouth, NH: Heinemann.

Graham, S., Berninger, V., and Fan, W. (2007). The structural relationship between writing attitude and writing achievement in first and third grade students. *Contemporary Educational Psychology, 32*(3), 516–536.

Heritage, M. (2008). *Learning progressions: Supporting instruction and formative assessment. CCSSO*. Washington, DC.

Schneider, M.C., Huff, K.L., Egan, K.L, Gaines, M.L., and Ferrara, S. (2013). Relationships among item cognitive complexity, contextual response demands, and item difficulty: Implications for achievement level descriptors. *Educational Assessment, 18*(2), 99–121.

Webb, N.L. (2005). *Web alignment tool (WAT): Training manual. Draft Version 1.1.*

Wisconsin Center for Education Research, Council of Chief State School Officers. Retrieved September 15, 2005, from www.wcer.wisc.edu/wat/index.aspx.

4

A Principled Approach to Performance Task Design

Performance tasks are measurement tools that teachers use to elicit authentic evidence of student thinking described in an SLO trajectory. That is, the teacher makes explicit the content difficulty, the contexts in which the child needs to *independently* demonstrate to show his or her knowledge, and the DOK level associated with each stage of thinking. For each of these stages, the teacher develops performance tasks to support learning and measuring those same skills. The development of tasks for each stage of the SLO learning trajectory results in a set of related, increasingly more complex performance tasks that the teacher uses to understand how a child is progressing over time to meet the intended SLO learning goal. In doing so, the teacher is using a principled approach to classroom assessment design and is making explicit his or her assumptions and interpretations of student work based on these tasks (Huff, Warner, and Schweid, 2016). Using a principled approach to classroom assessment design supports the validity of inferences about the student's achievement as well as the validity of the SLO process as a measure of student achievement gains across time. In this chapter, we focus on the third salient question a teacher must ask while creating the SLO framework for the year.

1. "What do I want my students to know?"
2. "How does student reasoning grow more sophisticated as a child learns?"
3. **"What progression of instructional and assessment tasks will support student learning and help me understand student thinking?"**
4. "What does each child already know?"
5. "What do I need to know about each of my students to support his or her learning?"
6. "How will I know that my students have reached their target?"

Overview of Performance Tasks

We started this chapter by stating performance tasks are measurement tools. What do they look like? Walk into classes and, if you visit at the right time, you might find

- third-grade students showing multiple ways to model a division problem
- fourth-grade students designing a science fair experiment on a topic of choice
- fifth-grade students writing opinion essays based on Scott O'Dell's *Sing Down the Moon*, a book about the forced relocation of the Navajo tribe
- sixth-grade students debating societal support of conformity as depicted in *A Wrinkle in Time* by Madeleine L'Engle
- seventh-grade students synthesizing oral histories about life during the Great Depression, with research and classroom learning providing historical context, as they write an article on the effects of the Great Depression on one of the following topics—families, government, migration, and society—for the class-developed newspaper from the time period

- eighth-grade students writing argumentative essays to support a claim regarding whether or not humans should be allowed to live in boundary locations that have a likelihood of future tectonic plate activity.

Brookhart (2015) defined a performance task as an assessment that

> (a) requires students to create a product or demonstrate a process, or both, and (b) uses observation and judgment based on clearly defined criteria to evaluate the qualities of student work (p. 3).

Swygert and Williamson (2006) wrote that a performance task should reflect the "evidence needed to support inferences about the examinees' knowledge, skills, and abilities." As you begin developing performance tasks you must determine if you need to draw evidence from a product or process. If your purpose is to determine, "Did the examinee reach the right conclusion?" (p. 301), then Swygert and Williamson noted a product-based task is appropriate. If your purpose is to determine, "Did the examinee get the right answer in the right way?" (p. 301) they noted a process-based task is appropriate. Another way to conceptualize the difference between the two is if an answer can be reached through multiple methods and these methods are acceptable as long as the correct outcome is reached, the task is product-based. If you are interested in measuring how the child is solving the problem or uses particular conceptualizations *during* the problem solving, then the task is process-based.

Process-based tasks are often temporal. That is, if a child is reading aloud and discovers an unfamiliar word, you watch the process the child uses to determine the word. Perhaps the child decodes the word, perhaps the child decodes the first syllable and then deduces the word based on the context of the sentence, perhaps the child skips the word to gain additional context before rereading the sentence with the correct word inserted, or perhaps the child stops to study the graphics near the text and notices there is a picture that begins with the same sound so that the child uses both context and illustration to infer the

Table 4.1 Examples of Product- and Process-Oriented Performance Tasks

Process	Products
Giving a speech	Poetry
Collaborating in a team	Script for a play
Delivering a newscast (Science Anchor, Arts Anchor)	Narrative, informational, and persuasive writing
Debating: strategies used	Journals
Read aloud	Webbing or concept maps
Improvisational dance	Propaganda posters
Safety in science labs	Scale model

Summarized and adapted from Green and Johnson (2010) and Kuhs, Johnson, Agruso, and Monrad (2001)

unfamiliar word. Such an event occurs in a time period, and once over, the performance no longer exists. It is best to capture evidence of the behavior with a recording mechanism (video or tape recorder), because when documenting one strategy you might miss another.

Table 4.1 shows examples of product-based and process-based performance tasks. Products include poems, play scripts, and concept maps. Student responses are static, that is poems do not dispel once the performance has been completed. In addition, for products the performance is not necessarily in a fixed setting. Students might develop their responses in the classroom or at home (although assessment tasks are optimally completed in the classroom). In contrast, for a process-based task, the teacher likely needs to be present during the event to observe the strategies or techniques the students use to solve a problem.

Designing Performance Tasks for SLOs

The development of a performance task for an SLO is informed by the content of the SLO learning goal, the SLO trajectory (The SLO ALD), and the cognitive demand (DOK) associated with the standards being measured at a particular stage of reasoning. In science, if the teacher's SLO learning goal is that Grade 8 students will create and interpret scientific information based on data presented in tables, bar graphs, line graphs, circle graphs, and scatterplots, he or she can measure the student's ability to interpret a line graph from a multiple-choice item. However, if the observable evidence in the trajectory discusses students organizing data, creating representations of data in graphs, and drawing conclusions this is best achieved through the use of a performance task.

Table 4.2 depicts the steps in developing linked performance tasks that serve to elicit evidence of growth along the SLO ALD. This depiction of growth is useful for the end-of-year conference you will have with your administrator as a component of the SLO process.

Table 4.2 Steps for Developing Linked Performance Tasks

Linked Performance Task Development Steps
1. Determine which stage of the SLO ALD you will first target. Review the SLO descriptor for the stage. Note the content difficulty, cognitive demand, and the context that must be elicited from the task. Document these pieces in the planning worksheet.
2. Borrow, adapt, or create the stimulus. Analyze the stimulus for complexity.
3. Create a task that is meaningful, motivational, and if possible connected to students' lives outside of school.
4. Determine the context of the task.
5. Determine the format (i.e., oral, demonstration, or product) of the final form of the student's response.
6. Address the degree of structure appropriate for the task.
7. Consider the logistics required to complete the task.
8. Write the students' task directions.
9. Review the task to ensure it reflects the diversity of the classroom.
10. Develop a continuum of tasks that contribute to the development of the skills in the SLO learning goal.

Step 1: Determine Which Stage of the SLO Trajectory to First Target

Document these pieces in the planning worksheet. You will typically want to create pairs of similar performance tasks for each stage of the trajectory. Therefore, you must decide the stage you will target first for performance task development. In this example, we will start with the Stage 4 descriptor.

Content Difficulty

In the Stage 4 descriptor of the trajectory, Grade 2 students write an informational text after listening to information from a Youtube video and reading information from a book. Optimally students can choose a topic of interest related to mammals, birds, amphibians, reptiles, fish, or insects. In this example, the student wanted to learn about bald eagles, so the directions were adapted for this purpose. Students can choose the topic that interests them based on preset tasks the teacher has already developed, or the teacher can quickly adapt preset task descriptions using appropriate texts and Youtube videos based on student interest. Because this task focuses on the writing process after listening to information from a Youtube video and a book multiple times, the task is moderately difficult because students are retrieving and organizing information across two different sources. In younger grades students are given time to synthesize the information, whereas in older grades students would be expected to engage in this process more quickly.

Cognitive Demand

When thinking about cognitive strategies that the student must demonstrate to respond to a prompt, two taxonomies for consideration include *A Taxonomy for Learning, Teaching, and Assessing: A Revision of Bloom's Taxonomy of Educational Objectives* (Anderson and Krathwohl, 2001) and Webb's Depth of Knowledge (Webb, Alt, Ely, and Vesperman, 2005). As seen in Figure 4.4, the revised Bloom's taxonomy has six cognitive levels, whereas Webb's DOK has four.

Table 4.3 Grade 2 SLO Trajectory

Stage 1	*Stage 2*	*Stage 3*	*Stage 4*	*Stage 5*
Students in this stage write roughly two simple sentences about a topic *from a digital stimulus (or book read aloud).* They present a list of facts or events that may be linked with the word "and." The order of sentences is not important. They demonstrate that words have syllables and must have a vowel when using inventive phonetic-based spelling. Students often use simple sentences to express thoughts using *either* a capital letter or a period.	Students in this stage use facts to write simple sentences on a topic *from digital sources (or book read aloud).* They present a list of facts or events that could be reordered without interfering with meaning. They primarily use simple sentences with correct sentence boundaries and high frequency one-syllable words to share information.	Students in this stage use related subtopic facts to write a paragraph on a topic gained from digital sources AND that an adult reads aloud. They group related details connected to the larger topic, however, grouped details could be reordered. They primarily use simple sentences with correct sentence boundaries, and on occasion, use a compound sentence. They apply first grade phonics rules accurately. They may introduce the topic or provide a brief conclusion.	Students in this stage write a paragraph based on information gained from digital sources and books they have read. They develop simple sentences (with and without compound verbs) and compound sentences that cannot be rearranged without altering meaning because they are beginning to use connecting words. They often apply second grade phonics rules accurately, such as r controlled vowels. They introduce the topic and provide a brief conclusion.	Students in this stage write complete paragraphs based on information gained across books they have read. The paragraphs may be reordered without interfering with meaning. They apply spelling rules such as r controlled vowels, vowel diphthongs, and early prefixes correctly.

Table 4.4 Edited from Hess' (2009a) Cognitive Rigor Matrix and Reading Curricular Examples

Revised Bloom's Taxonomy	Webb's DOK Level 1 Recall and Reproduce	Webb's DOK Level 2 Skills and Concepts	Webb's DOK Level 3 Strategic Thinking	Webb's DOK Level 4 Extended Thinking
Remember Retrieve or recall knowledge or facts from long-term memory	Define, locate, and identify facts, details, events, or ideas explicit in text Read with accuracy			
Understand Paraphrase, explain, summarize, generalize, illustrate, classify, categorize, infer a logical conclusion, predict, compare/contrast, construct models	Describe literary elements (characters, setting, sequence, etc.) Select appropriate words when meaning is explicit in text Describe who, what, where, when, or how	Explain or summarize concepts or why; show relationships; cause-effect Make inferences from texts, observations, prior knowledge Infer main ideas or make accurate generalizations from texts	Connect ideas using supporting evidence (quote or text reference), including how word choice, point of view, or bias may affect the readers' interpretation of a text Make inferences about explicit or implicit themes	Explain how concepts or ideas specifically relate to *other* content domains or concepts Develop generalizations of the results obtained or strategies used and apply them to new problem situations
Apply Carry out to an unfamiliar task	Use prefix/suffix/ word relationships (synonym/ antonym*) to determine word meaning	Use subtle context to determine word/ phrase meaning	Apply a concept in a new context justifying with evidence	Explain how multiple themes (historical, geographic, social) may be interrelated

Analyze Break into constituent parts, determine how parts relate, deconstruct (e.g., for bias or point of view)	Identify if explicit information is contained in graphic representations (e.g., map, chart, table, graph)	Analyze organization, and internal text structure (signal words, transitions, semantic cues) of different texts Identify characteristic text features; distinguish between genres	Use reasoning and evidence to support inferences and to analyze interrelationships among issues and problems Analyze author's craft to critique a text	Analyze multiple works by the same author or across genres, time periods, themes Gather, analyze, and organize multiple information sources Analyze discourse styles
Evaluate Make judgments based on criteria, check, detect inconsistencies or fallacies, judge, critique			Develop a logical argument for or critique conjectures with supporting evidence Compare and contrast solution methods against criteria	Apply understanding in a novel way, provide argument or justification for the application
Create Reorganize elements into new patterns/structures, generate, hypothesize, design, plan, produce			Synthesize information within one source or text Develop a complex model for a given situation	Synthesize information across multiple sources or texts Articulate a new voice

Table 4.5 Edited from Hess' (2009a) Cognitive Rigor Matrix and Writing Curricular Examples

Revised Bloom's Taxonomy	Webb's DOK Level 1 Recall and Reproduction	Webb's DOK Level 2 Skills and Concepts	Webb's DOK Level 3 Strategic Thinking/ Reasoning	Webb's DOK Level 4 Extended Thinking
Remember Retrieve or recall knowledge or facts from long-term memory	Write basic facts, details, events, or ideas explicit in text			
Understand Paraphrase, explain, summarize, generalize, illustrate, classify, categorize, infer a logical conclusion, predict, compare/contrast	Select appropriate words to use when intended meaning/definition is clear Write simple sentences	Explain or summarize concepts or why; cause-effect/organize ideas/make and support inferences Summarize main ideas or generalizations of texts	Connect ideas using supporting evidence (quote, example, text reference) Write multi-paragraph composition for specific purpose, and audience	Write multi-paragraph composition specifically relating information to other content domains or concepts with evidence
Apply Use a procedure in a given situation; carry out an unfamiliar task	Apply rules or use resources to edit specific spelling, grammar, punctuation, conventions, word use Apply basic formats for documenting sources	Use text features in writing Apply simple organizational structures (paragraph, sentence types) in writing	Revise for meaning or progression of ideas Use word choice, point of view, style and editing choices to impact readers' interpretation of a text	Illustrate how multiple themes (historical, geographic, social) may be interrelated with evidence in multi-paragraph composition

Analyze Break into constituent parts, determine how parts relate, deconstruct (e.g., for bias or point of view)	Decide which text structure is appropriate to audience and purpose	Compare literary elements, terms, facts, details, events Analyze format, organization, and internal text structure (signal words, transitions, semantic cues) of different texts	Apply tools of author's craft (literary devices, viewpoint, or potential dialogue) with intent Use reasoning, planning, and evidence to outline argument	Analyze multiple sources of evidence, or multiple works by the same author, or across genres, or time periods Gather and synthesize multiple information sources
Evaluate Make judgments based on criteria, check, detect inconsistencies or fallacies, judge, critique			Cite evidence and develop a logical argument for conjectures Compare solution methods Justify or critique conclusions	Evaluate relevancy, accuracy, and completeness of information from multiple sources Provide argument or justification for the application
Create Reorganize elements into new patterns/structures, generate, hypothesize, design, plan, produce			Develop a complex model for a given situation Develop an alternative solution	Synthesize information across multiple sources or texts to craft an argument and counterargument Articulate new knowledge or perspective

Table 4.6 Edited from Hess' (2009b) Cognitive Rigor Matrix and Math/Science Curricular Examples

Revised Bloom's Taxonomy	Webb's DOK Level 1 Recall and Reproduce	Webb's DOK Level 2 Skills and Concepts	Webb's DOK Level 3 Strategic Thinking	Webb's DOK Level 4 Extended Thinking
Remember Retrieve or recall knowledge or facts from long-term memory	Identify facts, principles, properties Recall conversions (e.g., customary and metric measures)			
Understand Paraphrase, explain, summarize, generalize, illustrate, classify, categorize, infer a logical conclusion, predict, compare/contrast, construct learning models	Evaluate an expression Solve a one-step problem Represent math relationships in words, pictures, or symbols Write and compare decimals in scientific notation	Explain steps, results, or concepts Predict from evidence (e.g., data) Generate hypotheses based on evidence Create models, graphs, or figures to represent/explain concepts	Use concepts to solve *non-routine* problems Connect ideas using supporting evidence Justify conjectures with evidence Show more than one response is possible	Relate concepts to other content areas/domains/concepts Develop generalizations of the results obtained and the strategies used (from investigation or readings) and apply them to new situations
Apply Use a procedure in a given situation; carry out an unfamiliar task	Calculate, measure, or apply a rule Apply algorithm or formula (e.g., area, perimeter) Solve linear equations Convert across representations	Use information from a table or graph to solve a problem requiring multiple steps Translate between tables, graphs, words, and symbolic notations	Design and conduct investigation for a specific research question Use concepts to solve nonroutine problems Show reasoning, planning and evidence	Determine approach forward among many alternatives Conduct a project that specifies a problem, identifies solution paths, solves the problem, and reports results

	Level 1	Level 2	Level 3	Level 4
Analyze Break into constituent parts, determine how parts relate, deconstruct (e.g., for bias or point of view)	Retrieve information from a table or graph Identify a pattern/trend	Classify materials, data, figures based on characteristics Compare/contrast figures or data Interpret data from a simple graph Extend a pattern	Compare interpretations within/ across complex data sets Analyze and draw conclusions from data, citing evidence Compare solution methods	Analyze multiple sources Analyze complex/abstract scientific concepts Gather, analyze, and evaluate information
Evaluate Make judgments based on criteria, detect inconsistencies or fallacies, judge, critique			Develop a logical argument for concepts or solutions with evidence Verify reasonableness of results	Gather, analyze, and evaluate information to draw conclusions
Create Reorganize elements into new patterns/structures, generate, hypothesize, design, plan, produce			Synthesize information within one data set Formulate an original problem/ develop model for a complex situation	Synthesize information across multiple sources/data sets Design a model to inform and solve a practical or abstract situation

For readers whose district or state uses the Webb DOK framework our task input for the Stage 4 descriptor is at a DOK 2. The task output, the writing sample, is a DOK 3 because students are organizing the information in writing and providing details (evidence). For readers whose district or state uses the revised Bloom's taxonomy the task input is understand and the output is apply because the task is familiar to students. By crossing the cognitive levels for the two taxonomies and providing examples, Hess (2009a, 2009b) formed a helpful matrix that allows you to translate a task or skill from one taxonomy to another. At the intersection of the two taxonomies within each cell are descriptors that describe observable behaviors. In the writing matrix, for example, students use word choice, point of view, and style at the apply level of Bloom's and the strategic thinking/reasoning level (DOK Level 3) of Webb. Thus, you can see where different aspects or traits fall when a student is able to demonstrate a particular skill, and use these tables as you construct trajectories and tasks. You are more likely to align with large-scale assessment expectations if your instruction and assessment go beyond the cognitive demand in the standards adopted by your district and state.

Context

Recall that context is the condition under which a child can demonstrate a particular skill. Context can include the degree of scaffolding the teacher needs to provide the student in terms of graphic organizers to support the organization of writing. Context also can be nuances in the content that effect the difficulty of the task such as the increments on a coordinate plane in mathematics or science. Context can be the separation of evidence in the text that is needed to draw a conclusion. In our SLO ALD, it is important to note that the child is allowed to choose the topic on which he or she writes. If this is the case, then we expect that the child is writing about an area in which he or she has high interest. This allows the teacher to see what the child can do when he or she is fully invested in a task. Central to context is also the reading demand of any text associated with

---

Monday

On the class iPad watch this video on bald eagles! You may watch this video Monday–Thursday.

www.youtube.com/watch?v=BEgEIEfSuvU

Next, read the book *The Bald Eagles* by Judith Jango-Cohen out loud for four days. Read to an adult, friend, or pet!

On Friday you will write an informational paragraph about bald eagles during class!

Friday

You have watched a video and read a book on bald eagles. Write a paragraph about this bird with information from your research.

Don't forget to include

- an introduction or hook,
- correct capitalization,
- correct punctuation,
- complete sentences,
- your spelling rules, and
- a conclusion!

Figure 4.1 Stage 4 Performance Task

the performance task. In our SLO ALD the Stage 4 informational text a child reads is the year-end exit goal for Grade 2 students. Each child will have multiple opportunities to read the book before having one class to write the paragraph. Thus, the Stage 4 task shown in Figure 4.1 is intended to be given in two parts: Part 1 Reading and Part 2 Writing. Students need to be given several days to complete Part 1.

Step 2: Create, Adapt, or Borrow the Stimulus; Analyze for Complexity

In considering the demands of a task, it is important to consider the task input in which the stimulus (also called the prompt) is a central component. The input, what specifically a child is asked to do, can influence the difficulty of the task based upon the content difficulty, the number of concepts or processes, or stimulus material students have to integrate to perform the task.

Task directions and stimulus often require the input of reading. However, for some tasks the input involves students listening, watching, or a combination of behaviors. In our SLO ALD, the input expectation is defined as *"information gained from digital sources and books they have read."* For this reason, we use a short video and an informational text the child reads independently. In Figure 4.1, both the video and the book are the stimulus material for the task.

As you create, adapt, or borrow a stimulus, you will need to determine the reading level that the stimulus materials should be for your content area. We recommend that the reading level for the Stage 4 (on track) be representative of summative expectations for the grade when the content area is reading, and the *Approaching Stage* representative of the mid-year reading level for the grade. However, if you teach a different content area and your goal is to measure content area knowledge, and not just reading, you will want to reduce the reading load in the performance tasks you create, perhaps to a grade level below that of your students. If the reading input for a task is too demanding, you will not know if a problematic student response in science or social studies, for example, is due to challenges in producing the required output or the reading demands.

There are multiple ways to analyze the reading demands of a stimulus. If the stimulus and student directions are in a Word Document, you can highlight the text you want leveled for readability, click on REVIEW, and then SPELLING AND GRAMMAR (this requires enabling "show readability statistics" under Word options and proofing in newer versions of Word). A pop-up window will ask if you want to check the rest of the document. Click on "NO." A new pop-up window will provide two types of readability indexes: the Flesch-Kincaid Grade Level and the Flesch Reading Ease.

For Grade 2, if you highlight the prompt and follow the steps above, a pop-up window provides a Flesch-Kincaid Grade Level index around 3.0. This means a second-grade student at *Stage 4* should have a stimulus with a reading load equivalent to a third-grade student just beginning the year. That is, a second-grade student at the end of the year should have the same abilities as a third-grade student at the beginning of the year. The other readability index, the Flesch Reading Ease, has a 100-point scale. As the score increases, the document is easier to read. With a score of 62.1, for example, a task is moderately-difficult to read. The scores for both readability indices are based on the average number of syllables per word and words per sentence. Technical language of the discipline (for example works like paragraph, informational, capitalize) will elevate the quantitative reading level above grade level. If you have taught your students to read these words, then having them in the directions is fine.

The Flesch-Kincaid, Flesch Reading Ease, and Lexile Measures are less sophisticated measures of text complexity because they rely on fewer text features to derive the text statistic. In elementary school, if students are reading short books you can often find the reading level of a book using either the Scholastic Website Book Wizard or the Lexile Web site. For middle school and high school materials, you can often get leveled text information on passages or texts you find on the internet or that you create or adapt by using free versions of text complexity tools. Examples include the ETS TextEvaluator tool (which provides information to help understand why a score is higher or lower) or an estimated Lexile level. This information will help you better understand and control the reading level required for your instructional and assessment performance tasks.

Step 3: Create Tasks That Are Meaningful, Motivational, and Connected to Real Life

Figure 4.2 provides data on student preferences for a television show. Once students are successful on the first task shown in Figure 4.2, the task in Figure 4.3 can be given, which is a more complex task in terms of content difficulty and DOK (Figure 4.3 is DOK 2 problem whereas the first figure is a DOK 1). In task 4.3 students must make a decision how to enter the problem and draw the conclusion that they must sum the number of students

The results of a class survey on whether students liked a new television show are as follows:

- 25 students like the new show.

- 15 students disliked the new show.

- 5 students had no opinion on the new show.

On the graph below, each 😊 represents students. Draw the correct number of faces to illustrate the results of the class survey.

😊 = 5 students

Liked	
Disiked	
No Opinion	

Figure 4.2 A Performance Task Tallying Student Preferences for a Television Show

across classes. Other topics that could be used might be favorite snacks, lunch food, music, book, and class subject. Notice that students who respond correctly to the first task can graph simple data by determining how many groups of five are needed when the data have already been summarized for them (children are given the sums for each category), whereas students who respond correctly to the second task are summing four one-and two-digit numbers and then determining how many groups of ten are needed. This is the beginning of creating linked performance tasks. Can you think of a more advanced task that students could do that target this same skill in a more sophisticated way?

One example of a potential Instructional Task 3 is Figure 4.4, in which children count and tally the representation of historical figures from different ethnic groups from a section of the media

FAVORITE ICE-CREAM FLAVORS OF FOURTH GRADERS

Class	Number Who Chose Vanilla	Number Who Chose Chocolate
Mr. Kennedy	6	12
Ms Ying	8	10
Mrs. Delgado	7	13
Mrs. Findley	9	15

The table lists the favorite ice-cream flavors of four classes of fourth graders. On the graph below, use one 😊 to represent 10 children. Draw the correct number of faces on the graph to show the favorite flavors of the fourth graders.

FAVORITE ICE-CREAM FLAVORS

Number Who Chose Vanilla	
Number Who Chose Chocolate	

😊 = 10 children

Figure 4.3 A Performance Task Tallying Favorite Ice-Cream Flavors

center's biographies. This example shows that instructional tasks can be group-based whereas assessment tasks should be a task a student completes independently.

When creating a task, consider whether the task can be used as a shell to create variations. Such is the case with the task in Figure 4.2, in which students vote on their favorite ice-cream (types of food and results could be modified) or in the task shown in Step 1. Examples of task shells are shown at the back of this chapter in Step 10 that align to the SLO ALD from Step 1.

Step 4: Determine Task Context

One touted benefit of performance tasks is the potential for providing a real-world context and connections outside the

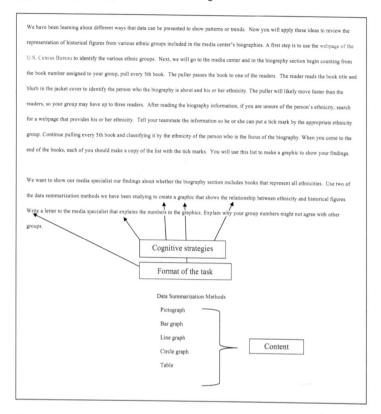

We have been learning about different ways that data can be presented to show patterns or trends. Now you will apply these ideas to review the representation of historical figures from various ethnic groups included in the media center's biographies. A first step is to use the webpage of the U.S. Census Bureau to identify the various ethnic groups. Next, we will go to the media center and in the biography section begin counting from the book number assigned to your group, pull every 5th book. The puller passes the book to one of the readers. The reader reads the book title and blurb in the jacket cover to identify the person who the biography is about and his or her ethnicity. The puller will likely move faster than the readers, so your group may have up to three readers. After reading the biography information, if you are unsure of the person's ethnicity, search for a webpage that provides his or her ethnicity. Tell your teammate the information so he or she can put a tick mark by the appropriate ethnicity group. Continue pulling every 5th book and classifying it by the ethnicity of the person who is the focus of the biography. When you come to the end of the books, each of you should make a copy of the list with the tick marks. You will use this list to make a graphic to show your findings.

We want to show our media specialist our findings about whether the biography section includes books that represent all ethnicities. Use two of the data summarization methods we have been studying to create a graphic that shows the relationship between ethnicity and historical figures. Write a letter to the media specialist that explains the numbers in the graphics. Explain why your group numbers might not agree with other groups.

Cognitive strategies

Format of the task

Data Summarization Methods

Pictograph
Bar graph
Line graph
Circle graph
Table

Content

Figure 4.4 An Instructional Performance Task Related to Data Representation

classroom. The context of the task in Figure 4.4 was from a mathematics unit on data representation. Students studied the use of graphs to summarize data, then they conducted a study of the ethnicity of historical figures in the biography section of the media center.

In the classroom setting, it is optimal to embed the task context in the theme of the learning unit (Kuhs et al., 2001). At times the context of a task is left open to student choice (Kuhs et. al, 2001). For example, the Common Core Standards include informational writing as an important genre for students to master. This type of writing provides students with the opportunity to determine the focus of their writing, or the teacher can focus the content on themes from a curriculum unit.

Step 5: Determine Final Response Format

Will the performance task engage the students in a process (i.e., an oral performance or demonstration) or elicit a product? In our Stage 4 task shown in Figure 4.1 the format of the performance task was a product: an informational paragraph. An example of an oral task is giving a speech and a demonstration task is an improvisational dance or improvised solo in a jazz band performance.

Step 6: Address Degree of Structure Appropriate for the Task

In the task shown in Figure 4.1 limited scaffolding was provided to support the process. A performance task can be highly structured through the use of scaffolding. Examples of scaffolding can include concept maps, outlines (e.g., Kuhs et al., 2001), or steps. When building in structure consider the DOK because when a teacher provides a great deal of scaffolding, it will be difficult to assess Webb's DOK Level 3 or 4. That is, Level 3 requires Strategic Thinking and Level 4 involves Extended Thinking. DOK Level 4 requires students to synthesize and make connections across multiple sources or conduct a project over an extended period of time independently. It is the *students* who should be making the connections. However, some students need scaffolding to help them be successful, especially when they are learning a new process, new content, or are in early stages of development. Figure 4.5 is a *Stage 2* task designed to support a transition from writing roughly two simple sentences about a topic from a digital stimulus (or book read aloud) to roughly a paragraph's worth of sentences. Less scaffolding over time and observable changes in student skills show growth.

Monday

On the class iPad log on to Raz-Kids and go to the level J books. Listen and follow along in the book *Tornadoes* by Keith and Sarah Kortemartin once each day Monday–Thursday.

Friday

You have listened and learned about tornadoes. Brainstorm four facts about tornadoes.

1.

2.

3.

4.

What is the most important thing you should remember if you are near a tornado?

5.

Now, write an informational paragraph about tornadoes with the beginning, middle and end. Don't forget to:

- capitalize
- punctuate
- use complete sentences

Figure 4.5 Stage 2 Task

Step 7: Consider Logistics Needed to Complete the Task

In considering the logistics for completing the task, think about the time needed to finish the task for 95 percent of your students. Your directions should specify supplies, resources, and time. Directions should also specify the place to finish the task—at home, in class, or a mix of both. In our task directions for Figure 4.1 and 4.5, students have four days to internalize the information in their book before writing their paragraph in the classroom. Also, review the IEPs/504s of students to ensure these students are considered in the logistics planning and to ensure any accommodations that are necessary are being considered. For example, some students may need to complete an assessment in a small group or have larger text.

An important, often overlooked, logistic is to determine when you will give the tasks. From school year to school year, the task associated with the SLO should be given at similar times. If you vary, for example, the timeframe of the pre-test across years your trend data may not be consistent. For example, consider if in the first year your SLO pre-test performance task was administered in late August and the evidence showed your students writing typically at a Stage 2 level. If at the end of the year your students show gains in the organization of ideas, variety in sentence style, and application of spelling rules and sentence boundaries (Stage 4) a year's worth of growth is evidenced. Perhaps in the following year you give the pre-test in late October, two months after school starts. The evidence shows your students writing typically at a Stage 3 level and by the end of the year your students' writing again grows to a Stage 4 level. In Year 2 less than a year's worth of growth is evidenced. Therefore, the results and timing of the pre-test might mislead your administrator into thinking that at the beginning of the year the students entered with more sophisticated writing skills than were actually present. Measurement of the students' true growth has been missed.

Step 8: Write Students' Task Directions

Elements to consider when writing task directions to students include (a.) task format, (b.) subject matter content, (c.) response mode, and (d.) evaluative criteria (Kuhs et. al, 2001). In addition, you should address logistics in the task directions. You should describe the process the students are to demonstrate or the product the students will produce. If the task directions simply require students to follow a series of directions (e.g., to conduct a science experiment) the task is reduced to a DOK 1. In the biography task (Figure 4.4), the content focuses on data summarization methods (e.g., data table, pictograph). The format of the task was a product in the form of a letter to the media specialist. The response modes include creating graphics and writing a letter to explain the graphics. The grading criteria are not, but should be, shared.

The *instructional* task in Figure 4.6 shows an example of best construction practice with directions written to the students. The task format is a product. The subject matter content elicited is an informational paragraph using science content. The response mode noted in the task is "write," and the student is told the evaluative criteria in the bullets. This task does several important things:

- The task requires students to use information they learned about and stored in their long-term memory as a central tool for responding to the task.
- The task elicits student thinking by having students integrate information across two stimuli in order to write the paragraph.
- The task uses authentic ways for students to access information, it connects learning to the world outside of the classroom, grading criteria are shared, and there is alignment to multiple content standards.
- The instructional task, as a result of scaffolded directions, elicits the grouping of related facts that is a key characteristic of Stage 3 on the trajectory. This task helps move a child in Stage 2 to Stage 3.

Analyze the *assessment* task in Figure 4.7. Once again, the task format is a product, and the subject matter content elicited is an informational paragraph using science content. The response mode noted in the paragraph is "write" and the student is told the evaluative criteria in the bullets. The task differs from the instructional task in that the scaffolded directions are removed to determine if the student can group related facts independently without the reminders. As the teacher, you can work to move students into a more advanced stage in a variety of ways. Here we show the use of scaffolded directions for instructional tasks. Another way to do this would be to remove the scaffolded directions in the instructional task and provide the needed scaffolding via instruction or one-on-one conferences.

Monday

Follow these directions for your morning work as soon as you come into the classroom this week.

Monday:

On the class iPad watch this video on dragonflies:
www.youtube.com/watch?v=A7hjkPknt_M

Tuesday

On the class iPad log on to Raz-Kids and go to the level L books. Listen to and follow along in the book *Dragonflies* by Cheryl Reifanyder.

Wednesday and Thursday

Choose to watch the video or listen to your book on dragonflies.

Friday

You have learned about dragonflies. Brainstorm facts about them and explain the information.

Fact 1

Explain:

Fact 2

Explain:

Fact 3.

Explain:

Highlight facts that are related and should be grouped together in your writing. Make sure to group these together in your paragraph.

Now, write a paragraph about dragonflies with a beginning, middle and end. Don't forget to:

- introduce your topic
- capitalize
- punctuate
- write a conclusion
- use complete simple and compound sentences

Figure 4.6 Stage 3 Instructional Task

Monday

Follow these directions for your morning work as soon as you come into the classroom this week.

Monday:

On your class iPad watch this video on frogs:
www.youtube.com/watch?v=Uja_QE4cZV0

Tuesday

On your class iPad log on to Raz-Kids and go to the level M books. Listen to and follow along in the book *Frogs and Toads* by Kira Freed.

Wednesday and Thursday:

Choose to watch the video or listen to your book on frogs.

Friday

You have learned about frogs this week. Now, write a paragraph about frogs with a beginning, middle and end. Don't forget to:

- introduce your topic
- capitalize
- punctuate
- write a conclusion
- use complete simple and compound sentences

Figure 4.7 Stage 3 Assessment Task

Step 9: Review the Task to Assure It Reflects Student Diversity

As we discussed earlier, a performance task is typically situated in a context. In developing a performance task a teacher should consider whether he sometimes includes some students (e.g., females) in establishing the context and other times uses others (e.g., males). Table 4.5 shows groups to review for accurate representation within stimulus and performance tasks for accuracy of depiction (Green and Johnson, 2010). In the right-hand column, we consider the depiction of the characters in the task in terms of behaviors, dress, environment, language, and physical appearance. The table can be used to guide a review either within a column or across columns. An example for the groups to review might include individuals in the upper levels of income (i.e., socioeconomic status). Do these depictions include African American, Asian, Hispanic, and white students? Are professionals (e.g., lawyers, medical doctors, financial advisors) depicted as male characters more often than females? An example from crossing the two columns could include the depiction of senior citizens (group) in a porch swing versus playing baseball (activity). Another example would be the use of an exaggerated southern accent for characters in a southern town. Another facet to consider is whether diversity is reflected in activities. Are any students in a wheelchair or with a prosthetic leg on the playground? Within Figure 4.8 only students with blond, black, and brown hair are represented. Who's missing? Students with red hair will know!

Study the table that shows the results of a survey of hair color.

HAIR COLOR SURVEY
RESULTS

Color of Hair	Percentage
Blond	17
Brown	50
Black	33
Totals	100

On the circle below, make a circle graph to illustrate the data in the table. Label each part of the circle graph with the correct hair color. Your grade will be based on correctly modeling each percentage and correctly applying labels.

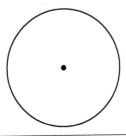

Figure 4.8 A Task That Omits Students with Red Hair

Table 4.7 Groups and Depictions to Review

Groups to Review for Representation	Review of Depiction
Abilities (e.g., physically disabled, gifted, average, mentally handicapped)	Activities
	Behaviors
Age (e.g., teenager, senior citizen)	Dress
Ethnicity	Environment
Family structure	Language
Geographic location	Physical appearance
Profession (pharmacist, teacher, medical doctor)	
Religion	
Setting (e.g., urban, suburban, rural)	
Sex	
Lesbian, gay, transgender, bisexual	
Socioeconomic status	
Language spoken in the home	

Return to Figure 4.3. In this task, diversity is reflected in the names of the teachers. The names appear to indicate different ethnicities and the sexes of the teachers include male and female. Among stereotypes to consider are males being depicted as better at mathematics and science, and females being portrayed as better at reading and writing. Such depictions are problematic when you often represent traditional roles rather than ensuring neither underrepresentation nor overrepresentation of depictions exists (Macmillan-McGraw Hill, 1993).

Step 10: Develop a Continuum of Tasks That Promote Development of SLO Skills

Our intended goal for this chapter is to guide you in developing a performance task for each stage of the SLO ALD. We also want to help you find ways to create tasks, when possible, to student interests. Although our sample tasks use Raz Kids to offer student choice, other sites such as www.pebblego.com can also offer similar types of personalized choices for reading. Websites such www.illustrativemathematics.org and http://achievethecore.org offer performance tasks opportunities that you can augment to create adaptivity in mathematics. For the

Stage 1 task we show a template that can be used to adapt to the child's choices.

We provided an SLO ALD and associated performance tasks aligned to each stage in Chapter 1 to show a continuum of tasks in mathematics. In this chapter, we first developed the task for *Stage 4* (found in Step 1). The *Stage 2* task is shown in Step 7, and the *Stage 3* task is shown in Step 9. Once one or two tasks are developed along the trajectory, you begin to see how you might create variations based upon student interest such as our *Stage 1* example shown in Figure 4.9. Recall the evidence for *Stage 1* says, "write roughly two simple sentences about a topic from a digital stimulus (or book read aloud). They present a list of facts or events that may be linked with the word 'and.' The order of sentences is not important. Students in Stage 1 demonstrate that words have syllables and must have a vowel

---

Monday

Follow these directions for your morning work as soon as you come into the classroom this week.

Monday:

On the class iPad log on to Raz-Kids level H. Choose one informational book to listen to three times this week. Follow the words while you listen. Write down your choice and show me.

Book name:

Thursday

You have learned about_____.

Now, write an informational paragraph in your composition book
about _____ with a beginning, middle and end.
Don't forget to:

- capitalize
- punctuate
- use complete sentences

Figure 4.9 Stage 1 Assessment Task

when using inventive phonetic-based spelling. Students often use simple sentences to express thoughts using either a capital letter or a period."

In contrast, students in *Stage 5* are expected to "write complete paragraphs based on information gained across books they have read. The paragraphs may be reordered without interfering with meaning. They apply spelling rules such as r controlled vowels, vowel diphthongs, and early prefixes correctly."

Scoring Guides

As part of the development of performance assessments a teacher may benefit from planning to score the students' responses if the task will also be used to give a student a grade. In such a case, a scoring guide (either a checklist or rubric) that specifies the desirable qualities in a response is optimal to create and provide to the student at the time the task is introduced such as the one shown in Table 4.8.

Exemplars should accompany the scoring guide (Johnson, Penny, and Gordon, 2009) to illustrate each level of performance. Exemplars can be developed over time as you collect student work across school years or by searching for student work examples on the internet. With each exemplar write a brief annotation that provides a rationale for the score to help you remember across time why you scored student work in a particular way. In addition to scoring, these tools—scoring guide, exemplars, and annotations—can be used with students as part of instruction. While the creation of scoring guides is beyond the scope of this book, interested readers may refer to the text *Put to the Test* (Kuhs et al., 2001) for guidance on developing these tools.

With the trajectory-based formative assessment SLO process, the SLO ALD descriptors may be considered similar to a rubric; however, there are substantive differences. The purpose of the trajectory is to describe the evidence a teacher should find in the student's work to infer that the student is in a particular developmental stage. The SLO ALD only describes what the student is doing. It is meant to describe when a student is able

Week 1

There are different groups of animals such as mammals, birds, amphibians, reptiles, fish, and insects. You will choose one animal to study. In the library, find two books on your animal. Show me your books so I can determine if they are just right for you.

Week 2

Read your two books each day to someone at home: a sister or brother, aunt, parent, friend, or pet. This can count as your home reading. When you are an expert on your animal, come and talk about your animal with me!

Week 3 and 4

You are going to write a report showing how much you know about your animal. Your report will have at least 6 paragraphs. Each day focus on the paragraph of the day shown below. When you finish a paragraph, check off that it is done below.

- ☐ What are the physical characteristics of your animal? (Monday)
- ☐ What are the body parts of your animal, and how do those parts help it survive? (Tuesday)
- ☐ Habitat – where does it live; and what is the habitat like? (Wednesday)
- ☐ What is the animal's life cycle? (Thursday)
- ☐ Introduction (Friday)
- ☐ Conclusion (Monday)
- ☐ Edit for spelling and punctuation (Tuesday)
- ☐ Identify simple and compound sentences. Place an S above simple sentences. Place a C above compound sentences (Wednesday)
- ☐ Neatly rewrite your report, and add a drawing of your animal! Turn it in. (Thursday/Friday)

Don't forget to include

- an introduction paragraph or hook,
- correct capitalization,
- correct punctuation,
- complete simple and compound sentences,
- your spelling rules and
- a conclusion paragraph!

Figure 4.10 Stage 5 Performance Task

Table 4.8 Sample Rubric

	Beginning	*Developing*	*Meeting*
Focus and control	You develop the topic, but lose focus because your details are not grouped together or are off topic	You develop the topic, but with uneven focus because your details are not always grouped together	You develop the topic, and maintain solid focus and control
Evidence and elaboration	You provide details to support topic but they may not be relevant for the paragraph. Can you highlight the details that best support each paragraph?	You provide appropriate details to support topic, but they are not fully developed. Can you highlight where you could add more information?	You provide appropriate and sufficient facts and details to support each paragraph
Conventions	You spell high-frequency words correctly, use some punctuation accurately with simple sentences. Can you find where you need to add punctuation and highlight this?	You use spelling patterns and apply the patterns when writing unknown words You form simple and some compound sentences with ending punctuation Highlight where simple sentences can be combined	You use advanced spelling patterns and apply the patterns in writing unknown words, form simple sentences, compound sentences, and use ending punctuation

to demonstrate the skill, and across stages it is meant to depict students' growth in reasoning as complexity is added to a series of inter-related performance tasks until the intent of the SLO "big idea" is met and exceeded. Optimally you can match and document multiple pieces of student work to the SLO ALD as evidence of the student's present level of performance across multiple occasions. The ALD can then support inferences about what the student needs to do next to grow from a metacognitive perspective. A rubric, on the other hand, is meant to describe the range of performance on a single task and often focuses as much on what students cannot do as what they can do.

For an SLO performance task, you might not wish to use a rubric because you can use the trajectory for this purpose. Alternatively, you may have an administrator who feels a rubric should accompany each task; thus, you must use your professional judgment. From our perspective, a scoring guide is not needed because the goal of the SLO process is to match the student work to the trajectory and then facilitate the student's move into the next level. Sometimes, the facilitation will mean targeting the student to specific instructional activities, sometimes, particularly for writing instruction, the facilitation will mean having the student revise work so it matches the descriptors for the next stage.

The SLO Performance Task Planning Sheet

To guide you in the process of creating your SLO performance tasks, complete the SLO Performance Task planning sheet shown in Figure 4.11. Once again, this planning sheet is intended to be a precursor task to completing the SLO template your state and/ or district requires as part of their documentation of the SLO.

Summary

Optimally, you will develop a related set of instructional and assessment tasks. At the beginning of the year you might need to administer one or more of the tasks as a pre-test. For many students, Stage 2 likely is appropriate as a starting point; however, for other students Stage 1, 3, or 4 might be the best place. You will have to use what you observe in the classroom and any other information you have to guide you. For example, if a child scored in the highest performance level on the previous year's state assessment, the Stage 3 task may be the appropriate starting

SLO Performance Task Planning Sheet

Grade Level	SLO Content Area

I. **SLO Learning Goal Final:** Copy and paste the SLO Learning Goal here.

II. **SLO ALD:** Copy and paste the trajectory here.

Stage 1	Stage 2	Stage 3	Stage 4	Stage 5

III. Determine which stage of the SLO ALD you will first target. Review the SLO descriptor for the stage. Note the content difficulty, cognitive demand, and context that must be elicited from the task. Document these pieces in the planning worksheet.

IV. Create, adapt, or borrow the stimulus. Analyze the stimulus for complexity. If the stimulus is text, document the text complexity here.

V. Create a task that is meaningful, motivational, and if possible connected to students' lives outside of school. Brainstorm how to connect the context of the task to students' lives outside of school. Not all tasks will be able to meet this ideal, but if you can, strive to. Brainstorm task contexts here.

VI. Determine the format (i.e., oral, demonstration, or product) of the final form of the student's response. Document the format here.

VII. Address the degree of structure appropriate for this task. Write a rationale for the amount of structure you plan to embed into the task. Document how you will lessen the structure over time.

Figure 4.11 SLO Performance Task Planning Sheet

May be photocopied for classroom use. ©2019 Schneider, M.C., & Johnson, R.L. *Using Formative Assessment to Support Student Learning Objectives.* New York: Routledge.

VIII. Consider the logistics required to complete the task. Where will you administer the task, and how long will students receive to complete each section. How will you address the needs of students who need additional time documented in 504s/IEPs? How will you address the needs of students who need other accommodations noted in their 504s and IEPs? Review each student's 504/IEP and determine what you need to do to support him or her. Document these considerations here.

IX. Review the task to ensure it reflects the diversity of the classroom. Document the considerations you made in your review.

X. Develop a continuum of tasks that contribute to the development of the skills in the SLO.

XI. **SLO Performance Task Criteria:** Compare each completed performance task to the following criteria.

✓ Your SLO tasks connect and integrate multiple critical standards that are central to the discipline within grade and intersect with standards in the previous and next subsequent grade in the beginning and advanced stages.
✓ Each task is clearly aligned to a stage on the trajectory and is clearly labeled to facilitate a comparison to the trajectory.
✓ Your task has least one stimulus.
✓ Your task directions are clear for the student and written using simple, noncomplex language.
✓ Your tasks are written are at DOK 2 and higher and go above the DOK levels of the standards at the later stages following the trajectory evidence.
✓ Students have sufficient room to respond on the paper, tasks are not cluttered, and font is at least 12 points for older students and 14 points for younger students.
✓ Underrepresentation or overrepresentation of different groups has been considered.

Figure 4.11 continued

place. At the end of the year, you will need to determine the optimal task to use as a post-test. During the year, give tasks when you determine a child is ready. Using both instructional tasks and parallel assessment tasks helps to support you in the process, and it gives a child multiple opportunities to practice complex, authentic, real-world thinking skills. If you want to see examples of high quality performance tasks you might browse Educators Evaluating Quality Instructional Products (www.achieve.org/EQuIP) for samples.

References

Anderson, L. and Krathwohl, D. (Eds.) (2001). *A taxonomy for learning, teaching, and assessing: A revision of Bloom's taxonomy of educational objectives (Abr. Ed.)*. New York: Longman.

Brookhart, S. (2015). *Performance assessment: Showing what students know and can do*. West Palm Beach, FL: Learning Sciences International.

Green, S. and Johnson, R. (2010). *Assessment is essential*. New York: McGraw-Hill.

Hess, K. (2009a). *Hess' cognitive rigor matrix and curricular examples: Applying Webb's depth-of-knowledge levels to Bloom's cognitive process dimensions – ELA*. Retrieved January 29, 2017, from www.nciea.org/sites/default/files/publications/CRM_ELA_KH11.pdf

Hess, K. (2009b). *Hess' cognitive rigor matrix and curricular examples: Applying Webb's depth-of-knowledge levels to Bloom's cognitive process dimensions – math/science*. Retrieved August 1, 2016, from www.nciea.org/sites/default/files/publications/CRM_math-sci_KH11.pdf

Huff, K., Warner, Z., and Schweid, J. (2016). Large-scale standards based assessments of educational achievement. In A.A. Rupp and J.P. Leighton, (Eds.) *The handbook of cognition assessment: Frameworks, methodologies, and applications*. Pp. 399–426. Hoboken, NJ: John Wiley & Sons.

Johnson, R., Penny, J., and Gordon, B. (2009). *Assessing performance: Developing, scoring, and validating performance tasks*. New York: Guilford Publications.

Kuhs, T., Johnson, R., Agruso, S., and Monrad, D. (2001). *Put to the test: Tools and techniques for classroom assessment*. Portsmouth, NH: Heinemann.

Macmillan-McGraw Hill (1993). *Reflecting diversity: Multicultural guidelines for educational publishing professionals*. New York: Author.

Swygert, K. and Williamson, D. (2006). Using performance tasks in credentialing tests. In S. Lane, M. Raymond, and T. Haladyna (Eds.) *Handbook of test development (2nd ed.)*. Pp. 294–312. New York: Routledge.

Webb, N.L., Alt, M., Ely, R., and Vesperman, B. (2005). *Web alignment tool (WAT): Training manual*. Madison, WI: University of Wisconsin. Wisconsin Center for Education Research.

5

Triangulating Evidence of Student Learning

Teachers can match different types of assessment evidence about student learning to descriptors found in the SLO ALD. This includes work from performance tasks, samples of student achievement from unit pre-tests or post-tests, and results from interim or summative tests. Optimally, a teacher uses information from multiple assessment sources to confirm that a student demonstrates the conceptual knowledge and skills representative of a particular stage of learning depicted in the trajectory.

During the pre-test phase, a teacher groups students into general categories of thinking within the content area: (a) early development, (b) typical development, and (c) more advanced development. Each group is administered a different task. For early development learners, a Stage 1 task maybe appropriate. For typical development, Stage 2 tasks may be warranted and for more advanced development, Stage 3 tasks may be the right starting location. The teacher will iteratively administer performance tasks from the trajectory so he or she can match the student work to a stage described in the SLO ALD. Individual students who do well on their first assigned task should receive the next hardest task. When students are unable to demonstrate knowledge on a starting task, they get the next easier one until a task the student is able to do successfully is found. This is the child's beginning point on the trajectory and is based on what the child can do. The next stage on the trajectory is what the child needs to learn and should inform the instruction that a student needs.

To identify the child's starting task, teachers can use results from large-scale assessments, scaled interim assessments, norm-referenced assessments, year-end work from the previous year, or beginning-of-year work from the current year to determine which performance task might be the best. Teachers who triangulate evidence use multiple data sources to draw conclusions about where students are in their learning to ensure that their own interpretations about a child's thinking can be confirmed. In this chapter, we will describe how to match a child's work to a trajectory. Next, we will show how the SLO ALDs can be used to suggest instruction to meet the needs of the child. Finally, we discuss considerations for using standardized assessments to triangulate teacher inferences about student thinking. In this chapter, we focus on the fourth, fifth, and sixth salient questions a teacher needs to ask while *using* the SLO framework during the year.

1. "What do I want my students to know?"
2. "How does student reasoning grow more sophisticated as a child learns?"
3. "What progression of instructional and assessment tasks will support student learning and help me understand student thinking?"
4. "What does each child already know?"
5. "What do I need to know about each of my students to support his or her learning?"
6. "How will I know that my students have reached their target?"

Matching Student Work to SLO ALDs

SLO achievement level descriptors (ALDs) describe the evidence teachers look for in student work to determine the child's present level of mastery and reasoning in the content area. The descriptor found in each stage of the trajectory provides the inference about the student's stage of development in relation to the big idea—the SLO learning goal.

When interpreting a student's response to a task, it is helpful to again examine the task to re-determine the content knowledge, the cognitive processes, and the contextual components that are intended to be activated. Next, look at what the student is doing as he or she responds to the task. (e.g., which descriptor on the trajectory most closely matches the knowledge and skills the student is demonstrating?). The matching of the student work to the most representative descriptor shows you what the child can do, i.e., the stage of reasoning the student has just completed.

There are three steps to matching student work to SLO ALDs. To gain the most from this section, we suggest you record your thinking in a format similar to Table 5.1:

Table 5.1 Example SLO ALD Matching Form

Student Name/ Task Level	What the child can do	The best SLO ALD match
Cliff/Beginning		
Maria/Beginning		

Steps to matching student work in this chapter to the SLO ALD from Chapter 1 include the following precursor tasks.

Step 1. Review the Grade 3 mathematics SLO ALD in Chapter 1 found in Figure 1.1.

Step 2. After studying the SLO ALD, investigate the samples of student work.

The first piece of student work in Figure 5.1 is from Cliff, a third-grade student. Ask yourself, "What knowledge and skills is this student demonstrating?" You should record what the child can do on an observational form similar to the one shown in Table 5.1.

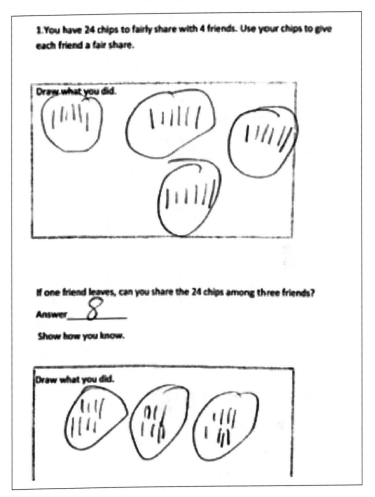

1. You have 24 chips to fairly share with 4 friends. Use your chips to give each friend a fair share.

Draw what you did.

If one friend leaves, can you share the 24 chips among three friends?

Answer ___8___

Show how you know.

Draw what you did.

Figure 5.1 Student Response to Task: Beginning Level

Next, study Table 5.2, which is a smaller portion of the SLO ALD from Chapter 1.

Step 3. Ask yourself, "Which descriptor most closely matches the knowledge and skills this student is demonstrating?" Record your observation.

Table 5.2 Sample of the Grade 3 Mathematics SLO ALD from Chapter 1

	Beginning	Developing	Approaching Target
Conceptualization	Equipartitions manipulatives of odd and even numbers (e.g., 27 divided in 3 groups; 24 divided in 4 groups) and explains equal or fair shares (Confrey et al., 2014)	Places manipulatives within 100 into arrays of more than two to model problems when prompted and explains (verbally or in written form) the relationship between repeated addition and multiplication	Self-creates models within 100 showing arrays to demonstrate the relationship between addition and multiplication

In this example, Cliff is equipartitioning a whole into repeated groups of equal size, which is one way to conceptually model multiplication and division. Cliff's work is a match to the beginning level of the trajectory, and he should be given the Developing task next. Let's look at Maria's response to the same task, illustrated in Figure 5.2.

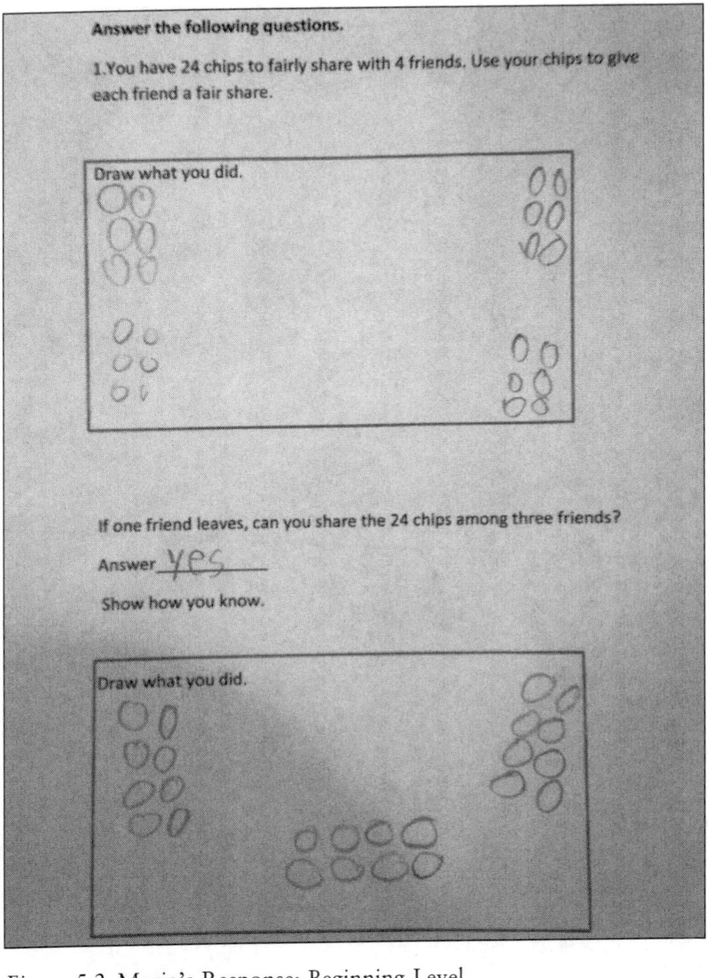

Figure 5.2 Maria's Response: Beginning Level

For the Beginning task for Maria ask yourself, "What knowledge and skills is Maria demonstrating?" Record your observation.

Next, ask yourself, "Which descriptor most closely matches the knowledge and skills Maria is demonstrating," and document in your records.

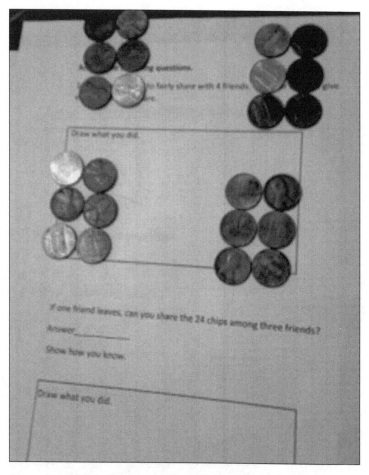

Figure 5.3 Maria's Response to Task: Beginning Level with Manipulatives

Maria is equipartitioning a whole into groups of equal size and formatting each of those groups into a 3×2 array on the first half of the task. This is a match to the Beginning level of the trajectory, and Maria needs to be given the Developing task next. However, Maria is *also* placing manipulatives into arrays to model a problem. Figure 5.3 shows how the teacher captures Maria's use of manipulatives.

Let's look at Cliff's work on the Developing task shown in Figure 5.4. "What knowledge and skills is Cliff demonstrating?" Record your observation.

Next, ask yourself, "Which descriptor most closely matches the knowledge and skills Cliff is demonstrating?" Once again

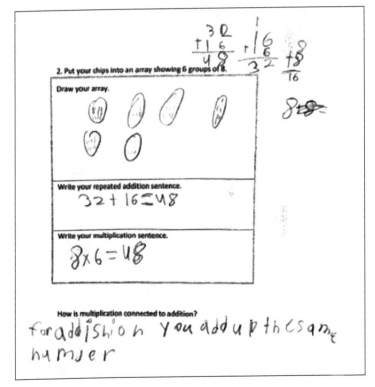

Figure 5.4 Cliff's Response to the Task: Developing Level

you will want to record your observations systematically to document your findings across time.

Cliff can model six groups of eight. He is connecting the model of the sum of the top part of the model (32) and the model of the bottom part (16) by adding groups of 8 (16+16; 8+8) so he is using an addition build up strategy to solve the multiplication problem. He can connect the multiplication sentence to the problem, but he is not yet modeling an array or explain-ing the connection between repeated addition to multiplication. Thus, with Task 1 and Task 2, we have two pieces of evidence that show Cliff is best matched to the Beginning stage of the trajectory, and he needs instructional support in the Developing stage. The Developing stage represents what he needs to learn next.

Cliff needs additional learning opportunities in conceptualizing multiplication as an array. Arrays are important precursors to creating area models (Battista, Clements, Arnoff, Battista, and Borrow, 1998; Confrey, 2012) and as such are an important foundation for the area standards found in Grade 3 and above in the Common Core as well as multiplicative thinking. Confrey noted that arrays can be thought of as showing the number of groups (rows) and the number within a group (column). Thus, Cliff needs to work with manipulatives to create the arrays, draw the arrays, and then to write the repeated addition and multi-plication sentence to support the connection that multiplication is repeated addition. This stage of the trajectory expands the Common Core second-grade standard 2.OA.C.4: "Use addition to find the total number of objects arranged in rectangular arrays with up to 5 rows and up to 5 columns, write an equation to express the total as a sum of equal addends" to model rectangular arrays, find the total number of objects in the array, and show the equation as the sum of equal addends and as the product of two whole numbers. It is not until students can model the row-by-column structure without manipulatives (Approaching Target) and show the connection of multiplication and addition that they should be encouraged to memorize multiplication facts.

Let's look at Maria's work on the Developing task. "What knowledge and skills is Maria demonstrating?" Record your observations about what Maria can do (Figure 5.5).

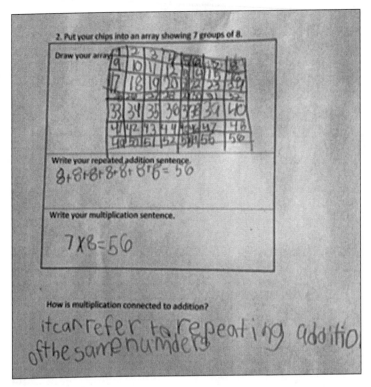

2. Put your chips into an array showing 7 groups of 8.

Draw your array.

Write your repeated addition sentence.

$8+8+8+8+8+8+8 = 56$

Write your multiplication sentence.

$7 \times 8 = 56$

How is multiplication connected to addition?

it can refer to repeating addition
of the same numbers

Figure 5.5 Maria's Response to Task: Developing Level

Once again ask yourself, "Which descriptor most closely matches the knowledge and skills Maria is demonstrating?"

Recall, when Maria responded to the Beginning task, she placed manipulatives into groups and within each group modeled an array. Maria was showing some evidence related to the Developing stage, but we needed to collect more evidence to confirm. Here, we see our thoughts are correct for two reasons. First, Maria is able to explain the relationship between repeated addition and multiplication. Second, she ignored the manipulatives and answered the problem using a self-created model. She then used the model to solve the multiplication problem. Once again, Maria seems to be operating between stages, teaching us some important lessons about interpreting student work.

Although we designed these tasks to elicit responses for a particular stage of conceptual understanding (i.e., Beginning, Developing, Approaching, etc.), children can often surprise us. If we focus on whether the student followed directions (in this instance Maria did not respond by using manipulatives) we might miss the thinking skills the child is demonstrating. It is the content area *thinking* skills we care about rather than if the child explicitly followed the intended directions. Maria's response has shown a clear match to placing manipulatives in arrays and a clear match to explaining the relationship between multiplication and addition. Her work has given a clear match for self-creating an array within 100. This is a threshold case (Ferrara and Lewis, 2012), in which the evidence alternates between adjacent stages of the trajectory. In such situations, a teacher makes the match based on which descriptor is the closest. In this case, we make the match to *Developing*, and we give her the Approaching task.

In the *Approaching* task, Maria could again model the array, but she did not model more common representations of equal groups of the same number. It is important that students have multiple strategies to solve problems; therefore, the teacher will want to find instructional activities that focus on different ways to represent the relationship between addition and multiplication. In this way, the teacher is differentiating instruction to the thinking skills with the content that are the foundation for the Approaching stage on this trajectory. Once the teacher believes Maria can self-create models showing multiple ways to conceptually represent multiplication and its underpinning of repeated addition, she can be given a *different* Approaching task. Maria can also be encouraged to begin memorizing multiplication facts.

The SLO ALD can help teachers think about how to differentiate instruction. In this scenario, the teacher is using the SLO ALD as a likely pathway to develop Maria's conceptual thinking skills in mathematics. Conceptual understanding will allow Maria to choose among multiple procedures to accurately solve novel complex problems by the end of the year. The teacher is using the SLO ALDs to support Maria's path to proficiency in Grade 3 mathematics, because this is what the SLO ALDs are intended to represent.

Using the SLO ALD to Support Differentiated Instruction

Recall the Chapter 4 SLO learning goal (students will use information from digital sources and multiple texts to write a complete paragraph on a topic of interest) and the SLO ALD. In Table 5.3 we show an excerpt from the SLO ALD, followed by an example of student work.

Read the student's response from the beginning of the year shown in Figure 5.6.

This second grader, Dylan, was able to use a hook to introduce a topic. He uses primarily simple sentences with the exception of the last sentence, which is a compound sentence. Dylan lists facts that could be interchangeable in arrangement and spells high frequency sight words correctly. Depending on the spelling curriculum used in a district, a second-grade student in the beginning of the year may or may not be expected to apply r-controlled

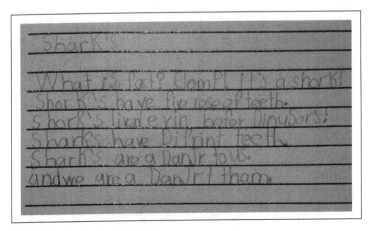

Figure 5.6 Original Student Response

Table 5.3 ALD Excerpt from Chapter 4

	Stage 1	Stage 2	Stage 3
Writing	Students in this stage write two or more simple sentences about a topic *from a digital stimulus (or book read aloud)*. They present a list of facts or events that may be linked with the word "and." The order of sentences are not important. They demonstrate that words have syllables and must have a vowel when using inventive phonetic-based spelling. Students often use simple sentences to express thoughts using *either* a capital letter or a period.	Students in this stage use facts to write simple sentences on a topic *from digital sources (or book read aloud)*. They present a list of facts or events that could be reordered without interfering with meaning. They primarily use simple sentences with correct sentence boundaries and high frequency one-syllable words to share information.	Students in this stage use related subtopic facts to write a paragraph on a topic gained from digital sources AND that an adult reads aloud. They group related details connected to the larger topic however grouped details could be reordered. They primarily use simple sentences with correct sentence boundaries, and on occasion, use a compound sentence. They apply first grade phonics rules accurately. They may introduce a topic or provide a brief conclusion.

vowels correctly; however, we see Dylan migrates from "or" to "ar" in shark later in the paragraph. Which descriptor most closely matches Dylan's response?

This is an example of a threshold case in which the evidence alternates between the Stage 2 and Stage 3 of the ALD. In such situations, as mentioned earlier, you make the match based on which descriptor is the *closest* to the student's work. Because the SLO ALDs can inform likely teacher and student actions that will support closing the gap between where the child is currently and the SLO learning goal, we are going to describe the collaborative interactions between Dylan and his teacher to illuminate one way this can be accomplished.

The salient purpose of writing is the communication of ideas. Dylan has written a list of facts or events that can be reordered without interfering with meaning after writing a hook to engage the reader. The teacher wants to assist Dylan's transition from writing a list of facts to grouping related details connected to the larger topic because the SLO ALD and the research literature upon which it is based suggest this would be the next more sophisticated stage in writing development. Dylan is already primarily using simple sentences with correct sentence boundaries (e.g., no sentence fragments, run-on sentences, and comma splices), and he already has a single compound sentence. He needs to make a determination whether "ar" or "or" lead to the correct spelling of shark. Because r-controlled vowels are noted in the SLO ALD, the teacher supports Dylan's encoding by helping him sound out the word. Because he appeals to his teacher in spelling the word "different" (another word with a r-controlled vowel), she helps him determine the number of syllables, and segment and isolate the consonant and vowel sounds to encode the word.

The teacher mentors Dylan in grouping related sentences. He recognizes that sentences about teeth should be grouped together, and returns to his desk to revise the paragraph as shown in Figure 5.7. At this point in the revision, Dylan's work most closely represents Stage 3 of the ALD. The teacher then decides that it is likely Dylan would be willing to do a final round of revisions.

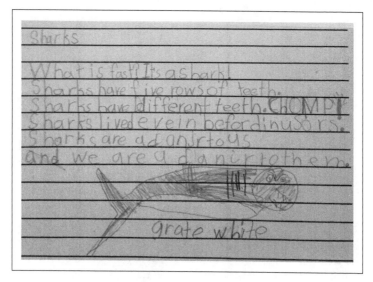

Figure 5.7 Dylan's First Revision

After praising Dylan for grouping related facts, the teacher asks him to read the paragraph out loud and find the sentence that seems most unrelated to teeth. Dylan responds, "Sharks lived even before dinosaurs." After agreeing, the teacher prompts him to think about why sharks need teeth, so Dylan returns to his seat and develops a new sentence as a replacement for the unrelated one.

Once Dylan has revised the essay again (Figure 5.8), we see his paragraph now most closely matches the Stage 4 descriptor: "They develop simple sentences (with and without compound verbs) and compound sentences that cannot be rearranged without altering meaning because they are beginning to use connecting words. They often apply second grade phonics rules accurately, such as r-controlled vowels. They introduce a topic and provide a brief conclusion."

We can see, based on the new illustrations, that Dylan understands the paragraph's focus on teeth, which suggests that he may be ready for the Stage 4 task found in Chapter 4 in Figure

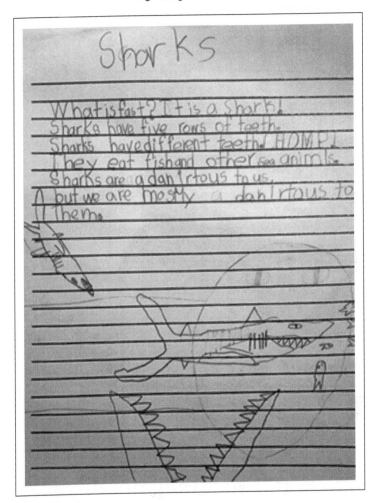

Figure 5.8 Dylan's Final Revision

4.1. Figure 5.9 shows Dylan's independent response from the mid-point of the year to a Stage 4 task. "What knowledge and skills is he demonstrating?"

Once again, Dylan uses a question to introduce a topic. He uses primarily simple sentences; however, he is also using two

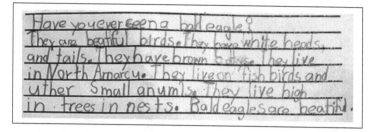

Figure 5.9 Dylan's Response to the Stage 4 Task from Chapter 4

direct objects in the third sentence, and writing a list in sentence six. Of import, Dylan is grouping subtopic related details (what bald eagles look like and how they live) connected to the larger topic, but the subtopics could be reordered. This shows that Dylan has moved from Stage 2 in September and is now matched to Stage 3 on the SLO ALD. Thus, we have evidence of growth!

With coaching and revision, the teacher can use the bald eagle paragraph to support Dylan's growth in writing, especially because this is a topic of high interest to him. Dylan's instructional level is Stage 4, that is, he needs to focus on developing the skills found in Stage 4. His teacher can coach him to write a descriptive paragraph on what bald eagles look like (and praise his use of a conclusion that bald eagles are beautiful) and then focus on coaching him on developing a second paragraph on how bald eagles live and the use of linking words. After working with him to obtain two complete paragraphs from this task with coaching, the teacher can create a *different* Stage 4 task to determine if he has mastered the skills noted in the SLO Stage 4 ALD. With continued focused coaching, the teacher can likely help Dylan transition and master Stage 4 during the winter. While this instructional example is shown for a single child, teachers can develop small group lessons for children in similar stages because they have similar needs. Teachers can help children in the same stage analyze each other's work as well.

The matching of threshold student work is complex. You have to rely on careful observation and analyze multiple facets of writing. Some students will have mastery over the communication of ideas and grouping of ideas but not on spelling or sentence boundaries. Students can be in different stages on different subdomains of the overall writing continuum or the same stage across subdomains. If divergent profiles are foundfor writing subdomains, it is optimal to break the subdomains apart so that student strengths may be noted and acknowledged in addition to opportunities for growth. This will allow you to document continued growth in areas of strength while simultaneously supporting areas in student writing that are in earlier stages of development.

Table 5.4 shows the Grade 2 SLO ALD from earlier in the chapter structured in a manner more similar to the mathematics ALD found in Chapter 1. When students have divergent profiles across subdomains separating the communication of ideas from the grammar and spelling is important.

Interpreting Summative Assessment Scores

Summative assessments, year-end large scale assessments administered by a state, determine how well students have performed on grade-level content compared to expectations regarding the amount of content students *should* have learned. Performance levels (also called achievement levels depending upon the state) are one of the main tools for interpreting test scores from summative assessments. Performance levels classify a student's test performance into one of several ordered evaluative categories (Haertel, 1999). For example, if a student's test performance is labeled Level 4 instead of Level 3, it implies that the student possesses a higher ability to reason and has more content area knowledge than her or his peers who scored Level 3 or below.

In the beginning of the year, teachers might examine aggregated previous year summative assessment results to understand how their students performed. Although some states encourage educators to analyze student performance on test subskills and use weaknesses in student subskill performance as the foundation for SLO learning goals, many statewide summative assessments are not created to support such score uses. To use summative

Table 5.4 SLO ALD Restructured

Writing Domains	Stage 1	Stage 2	Stage 3
Ideas	Students in this stage write two or more simple sentences about a topic *from a digital stimulus (or book read aloud)*. They present a list of facts or events that may be linked with the word "and." The order of sentences is not important.	Students in this stage use facts to write simple sentences on a topic *gained from digital sources (or book read aloud)*. They present a list of facts or events that could be reordered without interfering with meaning.	Students in this stage use related subtopic facts to write a paragraph on a topic gained from digital sources AND that an adult reads aloud. They group related details connected to the larger topic however grouped details could be reordered.
Sentence structure and spelling	They demonstrate that words have syllables and must have a vowel when using inventive phonetic-based spelling. Students often use simple sentences to express thoughts using *either* a capital letter or a period.	They primarily use simple sentences with correct sentence boundaries and high frequency one-syllable words to share information.	They primarily use simple sentences with correct sentence boundaries, and on occasion, use a compound sentence. They apply first grade phonics rules accurately. They may introduce a topic or provide a brief conclusion.

Table 5.5 Summative Assessment Elements to Review Before Using Subskill Scores

Element	Desirable Quality
Overall test length	The longer the test, within reason, the better
Number of subskill items	The more items that comprise subskill scores, the better
Test designed to support inferences at the subskill level	Developers use a statistical methodology described in a technical report to support interpreting subskill scores

assessment subskill information, teachers need to understand whether the test was designed to support inferences at the subskill level (see Table 5.5).

There are four guiding rules for whether it is appropriate to analyze and use subskill data on a summative assessment for SLO learning goal purposes. First, if the total test is relatively short (e.g., 30–49 items), only the total test score should be interpreted. Second, a fair number of items need to be used to measure a subskill to provide trustworthy information. Third, the test must be designed to provide subskill diagnostic information. Larger testing programs, such as the Partnership for Assessment of Readiness for College and Careers (PARCC, 2015), will specifically indicate on a score report if a subskill (or subclaim or subscore) should be interpreted. PARCC explains the interpretation of the subclaim is based upon the performance of the child compared to a reference group in that same category. Finally, if the subskill does not represent the appropriate grain size for an SLO learning goal only the total test score should be interpreted.

Performance Level Descriptors

States typically provide policy level descriptors to support interpretations for the performance labels they use for their assessment. These policy interpretations are then embedded into performance level descriptors that provide content-based interpretations for the meaning of test scores (Egan, Schneider, and Ferrara, 2012; Schneider and Egan, 2014; also known as range achievement level descriptors). Table 5.6 shows examples of policy level descriptors for testing programs in Utah and Georgia.

Policy performance level descriptors provide initial interpretations for summative assessment scores. In Table 5.6 both states describe Level 1 students as not meeting the expectations for the grade. These students, in general, are likely to be functioning below the targeted grade level and in the trajectory-based formative assessment SLO framework would be students for whom pre-test tasks in the beginning stages would likely be an appropriate starting point.

Students in the Level 3 areas of the summative assessment will likely need tasks at the Developing or Approaching Level of the SLO trajectory. Level 3 students have the necessary foundation to begin with tasks that are measuring early conceptual understanding of on-grade-level content. These inferences can be supported by reviewing the state's content based performance level descriptors for the summative assessment. There should be some degree of congruence between a teacher's SLO ALD and a state's content-based range performance level descriptors in those grades and subjects that are also measured by a summative assessment. It is important that teachers check their own SLO ALD to ensure it is not less rigorous than those proposed by their state summative assessment, particularly in regard to being "on track" or "advancing."

Interpreting Interim Assessment Scores

There are different types of interim assessment scores; however, across types, the reasons districts administer them are for three co-mingled purposes: (a) instruction, (b) program evaluation, and (c) prediction of scores on the summative year-end assessment (Perie, Marion, and Gong, 2009).

Table 5.6 Policy Level Descriptors from Utah and Georgia

State	Level 1	Level 2	Level 3	Level 4
Utah	The Level 1 student is below proficient in applying the mathematics knowledge/skills as specified in the Utah Core State Standards. The student generally performs significantly below the standard for their grade level, is likely able to partially access grade-level content and engage with higher-order thinking skills with extensive support	The Level 2 student is approaching proficient in applying the mathematics knowledge/skills as specified in the Utah Core State Standards. The student generally performs slightly below the standard for their grade level, is likely able to access grade-level content and engage in higher-order thinking skills with some independence and support	The Level 3 student is proficient in applying the mathematics knowledge/skills as specified in the Utah Core State Standards. The student generally performs at the standard for their grade level, is able to access grade level content, and engage in higher order thinking skills with some independence and minimal support	The Level 4 student is highly proficient in applying the mathematics knowledge/skills as specified in the Utah Core State Standards. The student generally performs significantly above the standard for their grade level, is able to access above grade level content, and engage in higher order thinking skills independently

Table 5.6 continued

State	Level 1	Level 2	Level 3	Level 4
Georgia	Beginning Learners do not yet demonstrate **proficiency** in the knowledge and skills necessary at this grade level/course of learning, as specified in Georgia's content standards. The students need substantial academic support to be prepared for the next grade level or course and to be on track for college and career readiness	Developing Learners **demonstrate partial proficiency** in the knowledge and skills necessary at this grade level/course of learning, as specified in Georgia's content standards. The students *need additional academic support* to ensure success in the next grade level or course and to be on track for college and career readiness	Proficient Learners **demonstrate proficiency** in the knowledge and skills necessary at this grade level/course of learning, as specified in Georgia's content standards. The students *are prepared* for the next grade level or course and are on track for college and career readiness	Distinguished Learners **demonstrate advanced proficiency** in the knowledge and skills necessary at this grade level/course of learning, as specified in Georgia's content standards. The students *are well prepared* for the next grade level or course and are well prepared for college and career readiness

Understanding Purpose

Teachers need to understand the intended purpose of the interim assessment in terms of how the assessment was designed. Some interim assessments are created to be a general survey of student knowledge and skill because the goal of the assessment is to inform teachers, parents, and students if the student is on track to meet proficiency targets by the end of the year. Such interim assessments fall into the prediction category of test purposes and are sometimes called mini-summative assessments. These assessments can be useful for helping teachers determine if it appears that more specific interventions need to be put into place for a child. For example, a child who is not predicted to meet state expectations for student performance and who is predicted to score on the lowest achievement level on the state assessments likely needs additional supports beyond typical classroom instruction. Any child who is predicted to score in the lowest level in a statewide assessment program is likely functioning in the curriculum below the targeted grade.

Mini-summative interim assessments can be good tools for baseline data collection. As the teacher is getting to know a child in the beginning of the year, he can use the interim assessment to confirm or disconfirm his analysis of student work. That is, are higher scoring students on SLO performance tasks also scoring higher on a predictive interim assessment? The interim assessment and the SLO performance tasks given at the beginning of the year can work together to inform a teacher's determination of a child's stage of learning in the curriculum.

Some interim assessments, called benchmark assessments, are created as a program evaluation tool to determine if the intended curriculum is being taught. Districts working to implement a standardized pacing guide often measure student learning against the pacing guide using benchmark assessments. These assessments are sometimes coupled with analyses to determine if students are predicted to meet state expectations for student performance.

Checking Content and Quality

Teachers need to be aware whether multiple-choice item distractors are developed to provide insight regarding student misconceptions. Goertz, Olah, and Riggan (2010) found multiple-choice distractors in interim assessments were not always based on student misconceptions, which limits their usefulness to a teacher in understanding student thinking. Thus, before using assessment results, teachers need to understand the purpose of the assessment design, check that the content that is administered to students matches the curriculum in their class, and identify the source of the distractor for multiple-choice items.

ELA teachers also need to ensure the passages that students are asked to read on any assessment are the longer, denser, more complex passages expected under the current college readiness standards in place across the United States. Because many state standards expect students to compare and contrast two or more passages, classroom assessments need to include this skill if it is not present on the interim. This expectation begins in late elementary school and above, and by middle school, this expectation is observable with primary source documents in history classes.

Interpreting Classroom Assessment Scores

When possible, teachers should analyze the conceptual issues that underpin items related to the standards. It is important that teachers contrast easy versus difficult items measuring *similar* content or the *same* standard to better determine what students did and did not understand and where student reasoning broke down. Item difficulty is the number of students who responded correctly divided by the total number of students who took the item. This information should then be compared against the SLO trajectory for similarities and differences on assessments measuring learning related to the SLO learning goal. For example, can students multiply when given well-posed, one-step problems but not when they have two-step problems that require strategic decision making? Can students retrieve explicit information from passages to support inferences or can they only retrieve such information when a question is literally answered in the text or when the explicit information is clustered more closely together? Can students find nuanced evidence that is separated across the passage or passages to support their inferences? These questions require analyzing both items and the stimulus material that students were requested to use to answer a question and comparing items from the same standards that are easy (many students answered correctly) and difficult (few students answered correctly).

Differentiating Instruction

Contrasting easier and more difficult items for students within a single standard reveals critical thinking disconnects and helps you determine the best option for instructional actions. For example, students who can respond correctly to well-posed, one-step problems that measure multiplication but miss two-step problems that require strategic decision making can be moved forward by having students work together to create and draw models of two-step problems. Students need multiple consistent opportunities to practice this skill. Finding real-world examples that can be given verbally one-on-one by the teacher can help you isolate if the breakdown in thinking is occurring when such problems are presented in any context, presented in print, or presented based upon more sophisticated mathematical concepts. One- versus two-step problem solving is central to understanding *when* a child can demonstrate the mathematical content knowledge they know. Notice the role of one-step versus two-step problems in the mathematics trajectory found in Chapter 1. Two (or more)-step problems requiring DOK 3 or DOK 4 thinking using the big idea of the grade level help you identify more advanced problem solving in children.

Defining Mastery

One important step in analyzing student responses to multiple-choice items or performance-task items is defining what it means to have students master the relevant skills found in state standards. Olah, Lawerence, and Riggan (2010) found that most teachers in their study identified mastery as 60 percent to 80 percent of students answering a particular item correctly. This definition of mastery is different from the statistical definition used when teachers define the minimum score on a summative assessment that students need to earn to be considered "College and Career Ready," as an example. A statistical definition of mastery is used in the Bookmark Standard Setting Procedure (Mitzel, Lewis, Patz, and Green, 2001), the most common standard setting method used for summative assessments.

In the Bookmark Standard Setting Procedure, teachers are asked to review multiple-choice items, student responses to constructed-response items, and student essay responses to writing tasks (if relevant) in sequence from easy to the most difficult. Thus, questions that 90 percent of students answered correctly are analyzed first and questions that only 15 percent of the students answered correctly are analyzed last. During the process the statistical definition of mastery means that 67 percent of students *with sufficient content knowledge* should answer the question correctly (as well as similar content). That is, the percentage of students answering the item is not the determining factor for mastery.

The difference between the classroom assessment process described by Olah, Lawerence, and Riggan (2010) and the summative assessment process is the classroom process is focused on the percentage of students who answer a question correctly and the summative assessment process is focused on the *content* that 67 percent of "College and Career Ready" students *should* answer correctly. The standard setting definition means you would expect students who have the prerequisite content-knowledge to answer a question with specific, particular content (for example two-step mathematics word problems that involve division) two out of three times correctly, or 67 percent of the time. The subtle difference between how teachers interpret mastery in the classroom and how they are asked to consider mastery during standard setting demonstrates the current disconnect in the educational field! On a summative assessment (and in the SLO trajectory process) we establish the content that defines what it means to be "on track" first. Then we say, if you are able to correctly answer difficult content, you have "mastered" the intent of the standards.

Merging Standardized and Classroom Assessments for Baseline Data Collection

Teachers must triangulate the content, the cognitive demand, and the context regarding what a student can do across assessment sources to get a broader perspective of a child's achievement. You must investigate the

- big picture in regard to what an assessment is telling you about a child,
- content the student is answering correctly *across assessment sources,*
- cognitive demand of the tasks in which the content is situated (what is the DOK level?), and
- conditions under which the child can demonstrate the content skills (applied mathematical problems, word problems, one-step or two-step?).

When you triangulate evidence of student learning across assessment sources you draw conclusions about student learning from multiple indicators. These different indicators should include summative assessments, interim assessments, and classroom assessments, when all are available. Not all content areas have such an array of assessments to support the triangulation process. Scores and feedback from other events in a discipline can also be used for this purpose. For example, students in performing ensembles often go to all-state auditions, solo and ensemble, and concert festivals. These rich sources of data from the previous year can and should be used to triangulate and support conclusions based upon samples of performances from within a performing ensemble class. To triangulate you must take the time to compare tasks measuring the same standards, determine the number of steps to respond to the problems from each source, analyze the DOK levels, and summarize what you know about the student's content skill and reasoning skill.

Summary

To monitor student thinking, analyze the task a student sees and their response, contrast student work on harder and easier tasks, and observe what the student can do. Matching student work from the SLO performance tasks to the SLO ALD can support instructional actions to move students forward in their learning. The SLO ALDs can suggest likely paths of instruction as students grow in their reasoning within the year.

Standardized assessments, such as summative and interim assessments, can be used to triangulate teacher inferences about student thinking. If a child is scoring higher on these assessments than on your classroom assessments, it can be an indicator you may be missing a student's sophisticated thinking or content skills or that other factors beyond the content are influencing his or her work in your class. When a student scores lower on these assessments than on your classroom assessments, consistently, it can be an indicator that your assessments are measuring different content or thinking skills. Matching student work to the trajectory, from SLO performance tasks and classroom assessments, can help teachers think holistically about where students are in their learning and support differentiating instruction to the needs of an individual child.

References

Battista, M.T., Clements, D.H., Arnoff, J., Battista, K., and Borrow, C.V. (1998). Students' spatial structuring of 2D array of squares. *Journal for Research in Mathematics Education, 29*(5), 503–532.

Confrey, J. (2012). Articulating a learning sciences foundation for learning trajectories in the CCSS-M. In Van Zoest, L.R., J.-J., and Kratky, J.L. (Eds.) *Proceedings of the 34th annual meeting of the North American Chapter of the International Group for the Psychology of Mathematics Education.* Pp. 2–20. Kalamazoo, MI: Western Michigan University.

Confrey, J., Maloney, A.P., Nguyen, K.H., and Rupp, A. (2014). Equipartitioning, a foundation for rational number reasoning: Elucidation of a Learning Trajectory. In A.P. Maloney, J. Confrey, and K.H. Neuyen (Eds.) *Learning over time: Learning trajectories in mathematics education.* Pp. 61–96. Charlotte, NC: Information Age Publishing.

Egan, K.L., Schneider, M.C., and Ferrara, S. (2012). Performance level descriptors: History, practice and a proposed framework. In G. Cizek (Ed.) *Setting performance standards: Foundations, methods, and innovations* (2nd ed.). Pp. 79–106. New York: Routledge.

Ferrara, S., and Lewis, D. (2012). The Item-Descriptor (ID) Matching method. In G. J. Cizek (Ed.) *Setting performance standards: Foundations, methods, and innovations* (2nd ed.). Pp. 255–282. New York: Routledge.

Goertz, M.E., Oláh, L.N., and Riggan, M. (2010). *From testing to teaching: The use of interim assessments in classroom instruction.* Philadelphia, PA: Consortium for Policy Research in Education.

Haertel, E.H. (1999). Validity arguments for high-stakes testing: In search of the evidence. *Educational Measurement: Issues and Practice, 18*(4), 5–9.

Mitzel, H.C., Lewis, D.M., Patz, R.J., and Green, D.R. (2001). The Bookmark procedure: Psychological perspectives. In G. J. Cizek (Ed.) *Setting performance standards: Concepts, methods, and perspectives.* Pp. 249–281. Mahwah, NJ: Lawrence Erlbaum Associates.

Olah, L., Lawrence, N., and Riggan, M. (2010). Learning to learn from benchmark assessment data: How teachers analyze results. *Peabody Journal of Education, 85*(2), 226–245.

Partnership for Assessment of Readiness for College and Careers (2015). *Parent guide to the PARCC score report.* Retrieved 7 May, 2018, from www.nj.gov/education/archive/assessment/parcc/resources/parents/Fall14Spring15SRIG.pdf

Perie, M., Marion, S., and Gong, B. (2009). Moving toward a comprehensive assessment system: A framework for considering interim assessments. *Educational Measurement: Issues and Practice, 28*, 5–13.

Schneider, M.C., and Egan, K. (2014). *A handbook for creating range and target performance level descriptors.* The National Center for the Improvement of Educational Assessment. Retrieved May 7, 2018, from www.nciea.org/sites/default/files/publications/Handbook_091914.pdf

6

Policy Decisions on the Use and Evaluation of Trajectory-based SLOs

To this point we have examined using formative assessment techniques, including embedded assessments, analyzing and interpreting student work, and differentiated instructional actions, to support the SLO process and make it more relevant to the daily interactions teachers have with students. In this chapter, we focus on the policy and infrastructure considerations that need to be in place for the intended purposes and uses of SLO data.

The SLO process is *not* a template that teachers complete at the beginning of the year and return to at the end of the year. It is a formative assessment process of understanding where students are in their learning and where they need to go next in regard to the SLO learning goal. The process relies on teachers (a) collecting accurate information from high quality assessments about what students can do throughout the year, (b) making correct inferences about what the student knows and can do based on the teacher analysis of his or her work, (c) providing

Table 6.1 Guiding Questions on the Use and Evaluation of
Trajectory-based SLOs

Guiding Questions
What policy decisions do I, as an administrator, need to make at the beginning of SLO process?
How do I determine if the SLO growth target a teacher has set is reasonable and attainable?
What are the key focal points for beginning, middle, and end of year SLO conferences?

instructionally appropriate feedback or instructional adaptations
for the student, and (d) monitoring students as they respond to
feedback or additional instruction to grow in his or her understanding of the learning target (Schneider and Gowan, 2013).

If you are an administrator, you need to know how to evaluate
the SLO process, but more important, you need to consider how
to support teachers in growing their own skills. Support is critical
because these are difficult tasks for teachers who have many
students, competing demands for their time, and many different
types of data about student learning to synthesize. What
resources need to be in place to make differentiated instruction
and record keeping easier for teachers? What resources need to
be in place to assist teachers in interpreting student work and
taking appropriate instructional actions? While we may focus on
the student-centered formative assessment process pieces of the
SLOs, the teachers will not forget that this process is centered in
evaluating their effectiveness. In this chapter, we help you answer
the questions in Table 6.1.

What Policy Decisions Do I Need to Make at the Beginning of the SLO Progress?

Professional Development Contact Hours

SLOs are designed to be a teaching and learning tool with multiple purposes. First, from a state and national policy perspective,

SLOs are often used as a student achievement measure with which to investigate teacher effectiveness. At a deeper level, however, SLOs are meant to encourage teachers to personalize instructional actions and tasks to the development of each student. That is, they are meant to activate teachers' formative assessment practices. Whether the SLO process goes beyond a compliance-based activity for teachers is often determined by how the administrator structures the process in the district or school and how much support and time the administrator gives teachers to learn and change their practices. Recall Gill, Bruch, and Booker (2013) recommended introducing SLOs as professional development and formative assessment prior to using them for evaluation.

At minimum, it will take a full year to construct the infrastructure and pilot the trajectory-based formative assessment SLO system, and a second full year for teachers to learn to engage in and integrate the process into the classroom.

In the first year, developing and piloting the big idea, the SLO ALD, and the progression-based tasks will by necessity be the focus early in the year and continue to be the focus much of the school year. Once this part of the process is complete, teachers need to improve their understanding of student reasoning by matching student work to the trajectory, developing resources to differentiate instruction, creating exemplars of student work matched to the trajectory, and tweaking the trajectory if needed. In the next section, we explore the administrator policy decisions that need to be in made in the beginning of the process to make the SLO rollout successful.

Individually Developed or Group-Developed Trajectories and Tasks

When implementing trajectory-based formative assessment SLOs, an important first step is to determine if it is optimal to have teachers create trajectory-based formative assessment SLOs on their own, in grade-level groups within a school, or have lead teachers do the work at the district level. We recommend having teachers work together on grade-level teams across the district because in our experience the teachers engage in the work most effectively together. (See Table 6.2 for a sample agenda for beginning the process with the assumption this book has been pre-read by teachers.)

Additional professional development time will be needed throughout the year so that teachers have time to match student work to the trajectory. Our experience is that early release days provide ample time for teachers, as a group, to discuss and match samples of student work to the trajectory and discuss next instructional steps for students in different stages of learning. Teachers can then return to their own classroom and match student work to the SLO ALD for their own students. It is important that teachers work together to develop consensus views about what student work at various stages looks like. The focus in Year 2 is integrating the process into the classroom and using it as it is envisioned under a full implementation, so teachers will administer tasks as they see students are ready throughout the year.

With teachers who are the sole instructor of their content area within a school (e.g., the music teacher, band director, visual art specialist, resource teacher) it is optimal to allow these teachers to work together across schools so that they benefit from sharing thoughts, and they see and hear the work of one another's students. The same is true for educators who teach students with significant cognitive disabilities. They will need time to determine how to integrate this process with a student's IEP goals, and they can review the National Center and State Collaborative (NCSC) instructional and assessment materials which are publicly available for support. Hess and Kearns (2011) supported development of learning progressions for this population. For teachers of English language learners or students in resource classrooms, it is important that they be paired with grade-level teams in content areas of interest. The focus in both the classroom and in the supporting program should be a single SLO that both teachers use and coordinate together to support an individual student's learning.

Table 6.2 Sample Two-Day Agenda for Creating Trajectory-based SLOs

Day	Time	Activity
Day 1	8:00 AM	Administrator Welcome and SLO Vision
	8:30 AM	Overview to SLO Structure and Policy Decision Points
	9:00 AM	Defining Big Ideas: Book Chapter Group Discussion
	9:30 AM	Study Grade Level Standards, Teachers work individually
	10:00 AM	Break
	10:15 AM	Define Big Ideas using Planning Sheet in Grade Level Teams
	11:00 AM	Groups Trade Big Ideas and Obtain Feedback
	12:00 PM	Lunch
	12:30 PM	Defining Big Ideas, Group Final Revision
	1:00 PM	Creating Trajectories – Book Chapter Group Discussion
	1:45 PM	Document across-year standards that to work together, to support the growth of the "big" idea" skill – Grade Level Teams using Trajectory Planning Sheet
	3:00 PM	End Day 1
Day 2	8:00 AM	Review Below Grade, On Grade, and Above Grade Curriculum Materials, Grade-Level Teams
	10:00 AM	Break
	10:15 AM	Sequence and Edit Standards, Grade-Level Team
	11:15 AM	Merge Standards into the Trajectory, Grade-Level Teams
	12:00 PM	Lunch
	12:30 PM	Creating Progression Based Tasks – Book Chapter Discussion
	1:00 PM	Determine stage of the SLO ALD to first target with Performance Task – Grade Level Teams Using Performance Tasks. Planning Sheet
	2:00 PM	Create First Task as a Group
	3:00 PM	End Day 2: Homework, each group member creates a task for a stage

Individually Matched or Group-Matched Student Work to Trajectories

In order for SLO ALDs to best support teachers they need to include examples of what student responses in each level look like (Furtak, 2009). The administrator needs to determine if it is best to have teachers match student work to the SLO ALD individually, with the administrator checking the matching process during the beginning-of-year SLO conference, or whether it is optimal to have teachers engage in the matching process across classrooms within a school or district. Furtak (2009) noted in her work that teachers may not always know the best instructional strategy for moving students up the progression; therefore, it is likely essential to have teachers work in groups to match student work and subsequently develop an array of instructional strategies to support differentiated instruction. This likely needs to be a focal area for the second year of implementation within a school. What strategies beyond what appear in the curriculum should the teachers also consider during reteaching for students who need additional opportunities to learn?

Differentiated Instructional Supports

As noted in Chapter 1, when teachers have a wide range of student abilities within the classroom (e.g., from the 5th to 95th percentile) they likely need digital curriculum resources to support differentiated and personalized learning for students who are in dramatically dissimilar and distinct learning stages. We know through research (e.g., Schneider and Meyer, 2012) that when teachers make one-size fits all instructional decisions, student achievement often decreases. If the trajectory-based formative assessment SLO process is implemented with fidelity, teachers will quickly desire and need *differentiated, personalized, digital* supports for students who are (a) one or more year's below-grade level, (b) on-grade level, and (c) above-grade level. Students learn at different rates, and decisions about how and when teachers move from grade-level to off-grade level need to be made and shared.

When a student's present level of performance is below grade level, the immediate focus of instruction can be on the prerequisite skills for the grade-level curriculum and the SLO learning goal. If a child has an IEP, the SLO information can be incorporated into the documentation with the next stage of development included as one of the child's IEP learning goals. However, not all children functioning off-grade have 504 plans and IEPs, so careful attention to matching instructional actions by the teacher and a second check by a curriculum specialist is warranted. For students who are functioning above grade level, we want to continue to advance them so their achievement does not stagnate; however, it is essential to ensure these students have mastered a large majority of the grade-level standards before doing so. With digital supports that are personalized to a student's needs, the acceleration of learning for all students begins. A district may need to release a Request for Proposals for such a vision and include teachers from across grades to review proposed materials and programs for alignment to standards and the trajectories being used to ensure coherence.

Infrastructure for Conferences and Student Growth Monitoring

The purpose of the SLO template designed by most states is to provide a beginning structure for thinking about student differences. States are largely silent on how teachers should set up systems throughout the year to monitor and adjust learning in regard to the SLO learning goal and how teachers should show evidence that they are differentiating instruction and assessments according to student needs. Teachers should likely develop a digital or paper-based portfolio to show evidence of how instruction and assessments changed for students in different stages of learning. Some teachers will copy the SLO ALD for each child and highlight the stage the child is at with a different color highlighter at different timepoints (see Figure 6.1), whereas others may indicate the month they matched student work to the SLO ALD stage (as shown in Figure 6.2).

	First Stage	Second Stage	Third Stage	Fourth Stage	Fifth Stage
Spelling Development	Uses physical representations (e.g., string of letters, scribbles) to write	Encodes to show 1 to 1 letter-sound correspondence for the beginning of words independently in authentic writing scenarios; may apply in a "sentence" or when labeling a drawing	Encodes similarly spelled CVC words during dictation and encodes first and last letter of CVC words independently in authentic writing scenarios. Shows phonetic awareness (e.g., MT for empty)	Encodes CVC words accurately and uses invented-phonetic spelling for words that are more complex independently in authentic writing scenarios	Encodes one syllable words with short vowel sound followed by –ck or with a double f,l,s,z independently in authentic writing scenarios and uses invented-phonetic spelling for words that are more complex
Print Concepts	Identifies whether a sentence needs a period and/or capital letter when prompted by the teacher in others' writing	Identifies whether a sentence needs a period and/or capital letter when prompted by the teacher in own writing	At times, applies capitals at the beginning of sentences and period marks accurately and shows awareness that words are separated by spaces	Applies capitals at the beginning of sentences and period marks accurately and almost always separates words with spaces	Applies question marks accurately and separates words with spaces
Communication	Draws to communicate a short personal idea with guidance and support	Draws and dictates to communicate a short personal idea with guidance and support	Communicates single thought/topic and will elaborate if prompted	Communicates single thought/topic and shows a connection or relationship between ideas using elaboration	Communicates single topic using a paragraph that includes an introduction and elaboration of multiple details

Figure 6.1 Tracking Individual Student Growth: Teacher Example 1

	First Stage	Second Stage	Third Stage	Fourth Stage	Fifth Stage
Spelling Development	Uses physical representations (e.g., string of letters, scribbles) to write **September October**	Encodes to show 1 to 1 letter-sound correspondence for the beginning of words independently in authentic writing scenarios; may apply in a "sentence" or when labeling a drawing **November**	Encodes similarly spelled CVC words during dictation and encodes first and last letter of CVC words independently in authentic writing scenarios. Shows phonetic awareness (e.g., MT for empty) **May**	Encodes CVC words accurately and uses invented-phonetic spelling for words that are more complex independently in authentic writing scenarios	Encodes one syllable words with short vowel sound followed by –ck or with a double f,l,s,z independently in authentic writing scenarios and uses invented-phonetic spelling for words that are more complex
Print Concepts	Identifies whether a sentence needs a period and/or capital letter when prompted by the teacher in others' writing **September October**	Identifies whether a sentence needs a period and/or capital letter when prompted by the teacher in own writing **December**	At times, applies capitals at the beginning of sentences and period marks accurately and shows awareness that words are separated by spaces **November May**	Applies capitals at the beginning of sentences and period marks accurately and almost always separates words with spaces	Applies question marks accurately and separates words with spaces
Communication	Draws to communicate a short personal idea with guidance and support **September**	Draws and dictates to communicate a short personal idea with guidance and support **October**	Communicates single thought/topic and will elaborate if prompted **November**	Communicates single thought/topic and shows a connection or relationship between ideas using elaboration **November December May**	Communicates single topic using a paragraph that includes an introduction and elaboration of multiple details

Figure 6.2 Tracking Individual Student Growth: Teacher Example 2

In each of these examples, the teachers used a common SLO learning goal and SLO ALD, kept track of each child, and made copies of the student work to include as evidence of growth in a portfolio. The student work served to support their match to the SLO ALD, but each teacher's own record keeping system was different. The differences in the teachers' record keeping system allowed each teacher to make meaning of the evidence in ways that worked for the individual, and both the record keeping system and SLO ALD showed evidence that the teacher was engaged in the process in the right ways.

Another approach is to ask teachers to carefully select samples of student work that represent students in different stages of learning if they are not comfortable collecting and maintaining work samples for all students. Based on the samples of student work that are different during a particular time frame (e.g., beginning of year), the teacher can write a reflection on what the students are doing, what they need next, and show evidence of lesson plans, websites, or applications they used to support the children in different stages of learning. They might use student work that shows an instructional action the teacher *did* take for students in the stage. From this perspective, the teacher uses the portfolio as a reflection point on how to differentiate instruction, and the administrator uses the portfolio as a window into a teacher's thinking about his or her own practice as student achievement is monitored. Under the latter model, the teacher would include the following elements in their portfolio in preparation for each conference:

- the completed SLO template from the state or district,
- the SLO ALD and tasks clearly labeled,
- examples of student work matched to different stages of the SLO ALD,
- evidence showing how he or she is maintaining records of student work in regard to the SLO learning goal,
- written reflections centered on student work matched to the SLO ALD describing what the different groups of students can do and what different groups of students need next, and

- evidence showing how instruction is being changed to the needs of the students (e.g., lesson plan, subsequent tasks, digital assignments, revisions, etc.).

How Do I Determine If the SLO Growth Target Is Reasonable and Attainable?

The decision-making framework for setting growth targets hinges on the SLO ALD used to help monitor student thinking. The SLO ALD describes emerging skills that students demonstrate as they learn. Another way to think of the descriptors for the SLO ALD is that they are related, interconnected sets of SLO growth targets. SLO growth targets for a year may be defined as moving up stages along the learning trajectory. Briggs et. al (2015), who supported and researched the implementation of a similar SLO approach with teachers in Colorado, found two levels of growth in one year to be feasible. Based on this research, moving up two stages on the SLO ALD is a reasonable starting point for the beginning of the year target.

Note in Figure 6.2 that the teacher matched the student work to the progression with annotations of the month in which a task was administered. The teacher matched the child's writing to On Target for the Writing domain in November, December, and at the end of the year. A similar profile occurs for grammar. From September to November the child moved up three levels; however, from December to the May the child's progress remained static.

This student is a good case study for the mid-year conference. Given the growth in the first half of the year, is it reasonable and attainable to readjust the child's growth target for the end of the year? For this child, it seems reasonable that instructionally the growth target of Above Target for two domains should now be the goal. The child has asynchronous development in punctuation, capitalization, and spelling compared to the child's ability to use drawing and sentence structure to express ideas. It is important that the teacher attend to all areas of development rather than shift to the weaker skill given that the child has met the original growth target (move up two levels) in one domain and exceeded in others. Administrators will want to encourage teachers to continue to develop students' skills even after they meet or exceed growth goals.

Key Focal Points for SLO Conferences

There are four important times during the year for conducting SLO conferences: before the beginning of the year, at the beginning of the year, at the middle of the year, and at the end of the year.

Before the Beginning Year Conference

It is helpful for a department head or curriculum specialist in each teacher's content area to spend time reviewing the SLO learning goal, SLO ALD, targeted standards, and the progression-based performance tasks prior to beginning the baseline or "pre-test" administration of the SLO process, especially in a large school. That is, prior to the beginning of the process, the SLO Learning Goal, SLO ALD, and progression-based tasks should be approved. These checks can be documented on the Planning Sheet located in this chapter. Once this is accomplished, the teacher can administer the first round of tasks, match student work to the trajectory, set growth targets, and complete the state or district SLO template information to prepare for the beginning of year conference.

Beginning of Year Conference

At the beginning-year conference teachers focus on understanding that students enter the year in different places in learning in relation to the big idea. The beginning of year check documented on the Planning Sheet located in this chapter supports these conversations. Notice we do not focus on group, individual, or tiered growth targets that are common across state SLO templates. This is because once a student has been matched to a stage on the SLO ALD, the growth target is to move the student up two stages on the progression. Each student's growth target is individualized. When a teacher aggregates the individual student information into common groups based upon the stages in the SLO ALD for the documentation of growth targets and instructional actions in the state or district SLO template, the teacher can indicate either individual or tiered growth targets—either is correct.

Consider this real-life example. A teacher has 17 students in a gifted and talented mathematics classroom. The teacher has identified that two students are in Stage 2 (Developing), 11 students are in Stage 3 (Approaching Target), two Students are in Stage 4 (On Target), and two students are in Stage 5 (Exceeding Target). The teacher sets the growth targets as shown in Table 6.3. How do you advise her?

This example outwardly matches the notion of tiered targets on state or district templates because different targets are set for groups of students in similar places of learning. Actually, the teacher is aggregating the data for reporting because the teacher has individual growth targets for each student based on the SLO ALD. This example shows an important point about what can happen in the beginning of year conference. The teacher has students across stages on the SLO ALD and has worked to find a solution for her gifted students at the upper end of the continuum.

In the SLO development process for Grade 3 students, the teachers who developed the trajectory identified five stages of development. However, for these gifted and talented students, 24 percent of the students were already at or above the intended year-end goals (Stage 4 and Stage 5), and the students do not have two levels to move up on the SLO ALD. In cases such as

Table 6.3 Example of Tiered Growth Target in an SLO Template That Needs Revision

Beginning Year Baseline	Number of Students	Growth Target
Stage 2	2	Stage 4
Stage 3	11	Stage 5
Stage 4	2	Stage 5
Stage 5	2	Stage 5

this, you likely need to pair the Grade 3 mathematics teacher with a Grade 4 mathematics teacher for support and access to an above-grade SLO. For the two students who at the beginning of the year are already in Stage 5 of the Grade 3 SLO, they need to be located on the most relevant Grade 4 SLO ALD to find their present level of content and reasoning development. The growth target needs to be adjusted with information from the Grade 4 SLO ALD. For the two students who at the beginning of the year are already in Stage 4 of the Grade 3 trajectory, they need to grow into Stage 5. When they have learned the concepts and skills from Stage 5, the teacher needs to locate them onto the same Grade 4 SLO ALD as the other two students. These students' growth targets need to be adjusted accordingly. These students should be case studies at the mid-year conference, because the teacher will need support to implement multiple curriculums in one class. Note this same issue can also occur in the inverse. That is, Grade 3 students whose work cannot be matched to Stage 1 may need to be placed on the next lower grade SLO continuum, with the expectation that they be given intensive interventions so that they may be moved back into the Grade 3 SLO after mastering the precursor skills.

Mid-Year Conference

At the mid-year conference teachers should be encouraged not only to show cases of students meeting expectations, but specifically to show work of those students who are behind and not moving forward sufficiently. Students who are on track for initial growth targets are those who have moved up one level on the SLO ALD by mid-year. The mid-year check documented on the Planning Sheet located in this chapter supports these conversations. Students who have either not moved forward or who have already met growth targets are important case studies for coaching conversations. These conversations ideally are based on how to support both the teacher and the students.

For those students at the mid-point of the year who have not moved up one level on the SLO ALD, it is not reasonable or appropriate to readjust the child's growth target for the end of the year. What is appropriate is investigating *why* a child is not moving up, determining if a child needs additional interventions, and determining if additional interventions are warranted that go beyond those a single teacher can be expected to provide. It is also important to note the percentage of students in the class who are not moving up at least one level on the trajectory. A significant number of students with such profiles might indicate that the teacher needs instructional coaching or is using instructional materials not sufficiently aligned to state standards and the district curriculum. The latter might be the case if a teacher has engaged in the SLO process independently, with little or no review from other experienced educators in the content area and grade. It is important to investigate quickly to provide the teacher with the needed supports to be successful by the year-end conference.

For those students who have met the growth target in the first half of the year, it is appropriate to readjust the child's growth target for the end of the year. It is simply not good for students to be static in their development for significant portions of the school year.

Year-End Conference

In preparation for the year-end conference it is important that both administrators and teachers understand the SLO business rules from the state in regard to which children are included in the growth target calculations (e.g., what dates students needed to be enrolled in the class by or the percentage of time a student was in attendance during the school year) and the last date teachers should collect evidence of student learning for the purpose of this process.

The year-end conference is the summative conference for the year. Therefore, student achievement data are entered into the state or district SLO template. The data are processed into a rating based on the state (or district) formula for student achievement of growth targets. There is not information for this step in the Planning Sheet because states will have different templates and processes for this phase of the SLO. It should be noted, however, it is critical to double check that all data entry is correct and calculations are accurate.

At the conclusion of the year it is important to determine the additional resources that teachers need to be more successful with this process in the subsequent year. Recall the expectation that this is a two-year implementation process. Teachers require a year to build the infrastructure and a year to practice using the process in the classroom so that it is integrated into their daily teaching. In year three teachers should be agile with the process, provided all the necessary supports have been put into place. Recall our earlier discussions in this chapter regarding the structure of the SLO portfolio and the need for digital curriculum supports to help teachers provide differentiated instruction to students in different stages of learning. These topic areas likely need to be considered each year in regard to what worked well and what additional supports need to be put into place. As teachers become more skilled in this process, an additional consideration will be if teachers are open to implementing more than one SLO learning goal within a single year.

Student Learning Objective (SLO) Administrator Review Planning Sheet

When using this worksheet (Figure 6.3) to review the teacher's SLO and provide signatures in a state's or district's SLO template it is important to remember that the template is a coversheet for the actual SLO process documentation. The SLO template, the SLO ALD, linked performance tasks, and student work evidence should all be considered together. The teacher should have an organizing structure such as a digital portfolio or a notebook for collecting and evaluating student work against the SLO ALD.

The following checks should be complete as a component of the SLO Evaluation process:

Sections I–IV are pre-implementation checks and should be complete prior to students beginning the school year. Section V is an implementation check and should be completed just before or as a component of the beginning of year conference. This step can occur in conjunction with the information placed in the state

SLO Performance Task Planning Sheet

Grade Level	SLO Content Area
Teacher Name:	Pre-Implementation SLO Reviewer:
SLO Beginning of Year Conference Reviewer:	SLO Mid-Year Conference Reviewer:

I. **SLO Learning Goal Criteria:** Compare the SLO learning goal to the following criteria. Place a check mark for those criteria that are met. All six criteria should be met in this section prior to beginning the SLO process with students.

☐ The SLO learning goal is measurable; it includes explicit, action verbs.

☐ The SLO learning goal requires that students engage in deep demonstrations of their thinking in the content area.

☐ The SLO learning goal contains the key content competencies a student should demonstrate by the end of the year.

☐ The SLO learning goal connects and integrates multiple critical standards that are central to the discipline. The teacher has evidence to support this claim documented.

☐ The SLO learning goal will elicit student reasoning at or above the cognitive demand levels denoted by single state standards in isolation.

☐ The SLO learning goal implies DOK 3 or DOK 4 thinking as being on track for the grade.

☐ The SLO learning goal grain size is appropriate to the amount of instructional time the teacher has with the students.

II. **Standards:** Review the SLO template. Place a check mark for those criteria that are met. Both criteria should be met in this section prior to beginning the SLO process with students.

☐ The teacher has documented standards that pertain to the SLO Learning Goal in the SLO template.

☐ There are multiple standards that are central to the content area and to the SLO Learning Goal in the SLO template.

Figure 6.3 Administrator Review Planning Sheet

III. **SLO ALD Criteria:** Compare the SLO ALD to the following criteria. Place a check mark for those criteria that are met. All seven criteria should be met in this section prior to beginning the SLO process with students.

☐ The SLO trajectory connects and integrates multiple critical standards that are central to the discipline within grade and intersects with standards in the previous and next subsequent grade in the beginning and advanced stages.

☐ The trajectory focuses on what students can do at each stage.

☐ The trajectory articulates evidence that students are increasing in content skill and critical thinking from one stage to another.

☐ The trajectory defines differences in content across stages rather than the frequency (e.g., no use of, often, sometimes, or counting) with which students respond to content.

☐ The trajectory describes the contextual or scaffolding characteristics needed so a student can demonstrate the skill.

☐ The trajectory increases in cognitive processing complexity across levels in a cogent way.

☐ The SLO trajectory implies DOK 3 or DOK 4 thinking as being on track for the grade.

☐ The trajectory provides a mental picture of increases in skill across levels.

IV. **SLO Performance Task Criteria:** Compare the SLO Tasks to the following criteria. Place a check mark for those criteria that are met. All seven criteria should be met in this section prior to beginning the SLO process with students.

☐ The set of SLO tasks connect and integrate multiple critical standards that are central to the discipline within grade and intersects with standards in the previous and next subsequent grade in the beginning and advanced stages.

☐ Each task is clearly aligned to a stage on the trajectory and is clearly labeled to facilitate a comparison to the trajectory.

☐ Each task has least one stimulus.

☐ Directions for each task are clear for the student, and written using simple, noncomplex language.

Figure 6.3 continued

☐ The set of tasks are written are at DOK 2 and higher and go above the DOK levels of the standards at the later stages following the trajectory evidence.

☐ Students have sufficient room to respond on the paper, tasks are not cluttered, and font is at least 12 points for older students and 14 points for younger students.

☐ Underrepresentation or overrepresentation of different groups in the text and graphics of the task have been considered.

V. **Beginning of Year Conference Student Work:** Review the Matching of Student Work to the SLO ALD. Place a check mark for those criteria that are met. All three criteria should be met in this section at the beginning of year conference.

☐ The teacher has administered and matched student work for all students to the SLO ALD.

☐ The teacher shows evidence of student work from the SLO tasks for at least three different students who are in different stages of learning.

☐ The teacher shows evidence of differentiating instruction for students in different stages of learning of the SLO Learning Goal.

VI. **Mid-Year Conference Student Work:** Review the Matching of Student Work to the SLO ALD. Place a check mark for those criteria that are met. All three criteria should be met in this section at the beginning of year conference.

☐ The teacher has administered and matched student work for all students to the SLO ALD.

☐ The teacher shows evidence of student work from the SLO tasks for at least three different students who are in different stages of learning.

☐ The teacher shows evidence of differentiating instruction for students in different stages of learning of the SLO Learning Goal.

☐ Students who have *not* moved up at least one level are identified and their beginning of year and mid-year work is present in the portfolio.

☐ These students should be a case study and additional interventions should be considered.

☐ Students who have moved up at least two levels are identified and their beginning of year and mid-year work is present in the portfolio.

☐ These students should be a case study and an increase in their growth target should be considered.

Figure 6.3 continued

or district SLO template for the beginning of year conference. Section VI is an implementation check and should be completed just before or as a component of the mid-year conference. This step can occur in conjunction with the information placed in the state or district SLO template for the mid-year conference. The year-end conference implementation check should be completed in the state or district SLO template.

Summary

In this chapter we focused on the policy and infrastructure considerations that need to be in place for successful implementation of the trajectory-based formative SLO process. The SLO process across the country is generally conceptualized as a template that teachers complete at the beginning of the year, followed by a year-end summary of student achievement of growth targets in the same template. The work of preparing to engage in the process and what happens between the two touchpoints with the SLO template has largely been undocumented. Much of what we have discussed in this book is intended to fill this gap.

Hopefully, we have made the case that the SLO process is, and primarily should be, conceptualized as formative assessment, centered in understanding where students are in their learning and where they need to go next in regard to SLO learning goals. We have demonstrated that not only does the SLO process necessitate substantial teacher skill in the collection, interpretation, and triangulation of evidence of student learning, but that trajectories (the SLO ALDs), coupled with progression-based tasks, can serve as a support system and infrastructure for this process. School administrators need to know how to organize and evaluate the SLO process, and to be aware of the skills teachers need to develop to engage in to be successful.

References

Briggs, D.C., Diaz-Bilello, E., Peck, F., Alzen, J., Chattergoon, R., and Johnson, R. (2015). *Using a learning progression framework to assess and evaluate student growth*. Center for Assessment, Design,

Research and Evaluation (CADRE) and National Center for the Improvement of Educational Assessment. Retrieved May 7, 2018, from www.colorado.edu/education/sites/default/files/attached-files/CADRE.CFA-StudentGrowthReport-ExecSumm-Final.pdf

Furtak, E.M. (2009). Toward learning progressions as teacher development tools. In A.C. Alonzo and A.W. Gotwals (Eds.) *Learning Progressions in Science Conference*. Retrieved May 7, 2018, from http://education.msu.edu/projects/leaps/proceedings/Default.html

Gill, B., Bruch, J., and Booker, K. (2013). *Using alternative student growth measures for evaluating teacher performance: What the literature says*. REL 2013-002. Regional Educational Laboratory Mid-Atlantic.

Hess, K. and Kearns, J. (2011). *Learning progressions frameworks designed for use with the Common Core State Standards in English Language Arts and Literacy K-12*. Lexington: University of Kentucky.

Schneider, M.C. and Gowan, P. (2013). Investigating teachers' skills in interpreting evidence of student learning. *Applied Measurement in Education, 26*(3) 191–204.

Schneider, M.C. and Meyer, J.P. (2012). Investigating the efficacy of a professional development program in formative classroom assessment in middle school English language arts and mathematics. *Journal of Multidisciplinary Evaluation, 8*(17) 1–24.

Index